D1607641

Moral Failure

Its Cause – Its Prevention

David H. Sorenson, D. Min.

Northstar Ministries
Duluth, MN, USA

Library of Congress Control Number: 2007926475
ISBN: 978-0-9711384-2-1

Northstar Baptist Ministries
1820 West Morgan Street
Duluth, MN 55811-1878

davidsorenson@juno.com
http://www.northstarministries.com

TABLE OF CONTENTS

Chapters

Foreword

The scandals concerning Jim Baker and Jimmy Swaggart broke when I was just a young man headed toward the ministry. The shame that it brought to the name of Christ and the barriers it erected in witnessing to the lost remain fresh on my mind. That was in the late 1980s and those men were far from independent Baptists. Sadly, since that time, numbers of preachers within our own ranks have fallen prey to immorality and thus disqualified themselves from the preaching and leadership ministry to which they were called.

Moral Failure, has been written for such a time as this. Those who read its contents will find first that it meets a *desperate need*! The inspired indictment of Jeremiah rings with alarming relevance, "I have seen also in the prophets of Jerusalem an horrible thing: they commit adultery…" (Jeremiah 23:14). When preachers are resigning because of internet pornography, a one time sexual escapade, secret affairs, or years of abominable sin, there is without question a desperate need! *Moral Failure* meets that need.

The readers of these sobering words will also discover the value of Dr. Sorenson's work in that it gives a *scriptural solution*. Sometimes, when presenting this subject, various authors have sought to lead the reader down the path of complicated psychology, clever wit, theoretical measures, and human remedies. These frail ideas only lead to frustration and failure. The Bible is the answer! It is "profitable for doctrine, for reproof, for correction, for instruction in righteousness: That *the man of God* may be perfect, throughly furnished unto all good works" (II Timothy 3:16-17). *Moral Failure* will drive home the simple truths that consuming God's Word in large doses and yielding to God's Spirit each moment will prevent one from falling into Satan's snare.

Mostly, each one who reads these potent pages will note that it comes from a *godly source.* The blameless testimony of Pastor David Sorenson throughout his many years in the ministry bears this out. Men and ladies from Florida to Illinois to Minnesota, and throughout the world, can testify to his Spirit-filled life. I have spent time in his home, have had the privilege of preaching in his church on more than one occasion, and can personally bear witness to his godly manner and impeccable character. He is not one who preaches high and lives low. Instead, his life has born and continues to bear record to the truth!

One has said, "An ounce of prevention is worth a pound of cure." That is the essence of this book. The biblical, simple, and yet practical admonishment found within will arm God's soldiers, indeed, with a powerful ounce of prevention! I urge each reader, for the cause of Jesus Christ, to eagerly devour the wisdom that will ensue. Diligently meditate upon the Word that will be given.Then, immediately apply the truths that will be discovered. It is my prayer that God will mightily use this book to keep another preacher from falling over the precipice and into moral failure!

Evangelist Dwight M. Smith

Introduction

As I sit down to write another book, my heart aches over news received recently of another good man in God's work who has had moral failure. Over the years, as God has allowed me to write, most frequently something has come to pass which became a catalyst for writing. Years ago, a missionary friend sat in our home with his family. After they left, I said to my wife, "They are going to have trouble with their children." That prophecy unfortunately came to pass and that good man is no longer on the mission field as a result. That event was the catalyst of writing the book *Training Your Children to Turn out Right* back in 1994.

When my father died in 1996, it proved to be a catalyst for writing the book *The Art of Pastoring* which in considerable measure was an overview of his philosophy of pastoring. Realizing the need for godly wisdom in young adults prompted me several years ago to publish *The Proverbs – Godly Advice for Young Adults.*

Today as I begin to write this book, the recent news of a pastor friend who was forced to resign his prominent church because of moral failure is the catalyst to write once again. I believe that God has given insights to me in this regard which can be a benefit for people serving God whether they be young or old.

I have been saved for over forty years. I have been in the ministry in one way or another for more than thirty seven of those years. Over the decades, there has been a steady stream of preachers – both small and great – who have had a moral failure in their lives which forced them out of the ministry. Sadly, the frequency thereof seems to be increasing. As I have been a bystander thereto, I have witnessed patterns which seem to be similar in many of the sad situations. I do not consider myself better than any other nor do I have all the answers.

However, in this book will be found a number of basic biblical principles which if followed, I believe, will keep God's people from falling. They are not new and they are not complicated. Sadly, good men (and women) often deviate from the basics of the Christian life. In so doing, they make themselves targets for the evil one. It is my hope that this book can help others to avoid the sad and ignominious end that many of God's people have found when moral failure crept into their lives.

I realize that in writing and publishing such a book, I will make myself a target of criticism and disdain by some. So be it. However, as I have sensed the Lord's leading in the writing of other books, I have sensed that leading again. It has been some years since I sat down and wrote a new book and I wondered if or when I would do so in the future. But the news of a fallen friend has stirred me to write once again. I believe that stirring is from the Chief Shepherd. I hereby dedicate this book to help good men and women avoid the ignominious end of moral failure in their lives and ministries.

David Sorenson
Northstar Ministries

* * * * *

The Apostle Paul wrote of the "high calling of God in Christ Jesus."[1] A man whom Jesus Christ has called into His ministry indeed has a high calling. There is no higher calling. Whether he becomes a pastor, an evangelist, a missionary, or eventually becomes the president of an institution of Christian higher learning, a man in the ministry is in a place of honor. However, with that honor comes a great responsibility. He must be and remain above reproach. Furthermore, unto whom much is given, much shall be required.[2] Accordingly, the Holy Spirit so directed the Apostle to inscripturate specific qualifications and criteria for one in spiritual leadership. The qualifications of I Timothy 3 and Titus 1 refer specifically to the office of pastor. However, in the view of this commentator, they surely apply to any man in a God-given role of spiritual leadership.

> *"A bishop then must be blameless, the husband of one wife, vigilant, sober, of good behaviour, given to hospitality, apt to teach; Not given to wine, no striker, not greedy of filthy lucre; but patient, not a brawler, not covetous; One that ruleth well his own house, having his children in subjection with all gravity; (For if a man know not how to rule his own house, how shall he take care of the church of God?) Not a novice, lest being lifted up with pride he fall into the condemnation of the devil. Moreover he must have a good report of them which are without; lest he fall into reproach and the snare of the devil."*[3]

Notice that the first qualification of a bishop (i.e., pastor) is that he must be blameless. Then notice also that the concluding criteria for a pastor is that "*he must have a good report of them which are without; lest he fall into reproach and the snare of the devil.*" These two qualifications are like book ends for one in spiritual leadership: being blameless and without reproach. A spiritual leader who is an adulterer is no longer blameless. Likewise, one who has a habit of viewing pornography no longer is of good report.

Solomon wrote long ago, "*Dead flies cause the ointment of the apothecary to send forth a stinking savour: so doth a little folly him that is in reputation for wisdom and honour.*"[4] The idea is of an old-fashioned pharmacist making up an expensive ointment for medicinal use. To find dead flies therein would be repugnant. The thought is of finding dead flies in a prescription purchased at a pharmacy. The inspired text thence describes how one in a position of wisdom and honor (i.e., spiritual leadership) is viewed when found with folly in his life.

The concept of folly in the Old Testament has the sense of evil foolishness or sinful foolishness. Such is an apt description of moral failure. It is wrong and it is stupid. Accordingly, even as a dead insect in pharmaceutical preparation is repugnant, so is sexual sin in a spiritual leader. A prescription with a dead bug in it will be rejected; so is a spiritual leader with moral failure. He is no longer blameless or above reproach.

Even in the sinful world in which we live, sexual sin in the lives of those in prominent positions is viewed as wrong. The world may snicker over adultery or the sexual "peccadilloes" of others, but they still take a dim view of such behavior of those assumed to be respectable. Should a school superintendent be found committing adultery or using hard-core pornography, in most places, his days will be numbered. Though he may not be arrested, still his position in that community will soon be over. Notwithstanding the coverup of President Clinton's sexual sin for political reasons, the career of most lessor elected officials may soon be over when they are found guilty of open adultery or using pornography while in office. If that be the case for secular officials, how much more so for a man of God?

A deacon in our church related to me a story of an event which he witnessed several years ago. At the time, he was an aircraft inspector for a major airline. Company policy forbad employees from using company computers to access internet pornography at work.[5] One day, a fellow employee was caught viewing pornography online while on duty. He was fired on the spot and unceremoniously escorted off the property by security personnel. If secular corporations have such policies, how much more ought one in spiritual leadership be above reproach in this regard? Though the business world may have different motives for prohibiting pornography in the workplace, nevertheless, the bottom line is they know it is wrong. When a spiritual leader gets involved therewith, he pretty well dissolves his moral authority and influence. He no longer is blameless.

Moreover, in Paul's epistle to Titus regarding qualifications for the ministry, the criteria of being blameless appears twice.[6] The bottom line is that when a spiritual leader ventures into the realm of sexual sin, he is no longer blameless. God will forgive such sin on a personal basis when repentance and confession are accomplished. However, the qualification of being blameless has been broken like a piece of glass. Like Humpty Dumpty of old, the pieces can never be assembled again.

Sexual sin is something which will follow a person for years thereafter. One can tell a lie and before long it will be forgotten. One might even be less than honest in business dealings and it eventually will fade from view. However, an adulterer will always be known as an adulterer even as a murderer will always be known as a murderer, especially in Christian circles. God may forgive one of such sin upon repentance and confession, but the reputation will long endure.

Onc guilty of sexual sin will render himself disqualified for the ministry not only for scriptural reasons, but for practical reasons as well. The reputation and knowledge of such will linger for many years, if not forever. That is sad, but it is the truth. The devil knows that as well. He therefore seeks to snare those in spiritual leadership, knowing that he will neutralize a servant of God. God therefore was infinitely wise when he set forth the criteria of blamelessness for those in spiritual leadership. Such is necessary for leadership in God's work.

Chapter Notes

[1]Philippians 3:14

[2]Luke 12:48

[3]I Timothy 3:2-7

[4]Ecclesiastes 10:1

[5]This probably had more to do with avoiding sexual harassment issues as well as wasting company time while on duty. Nevertheless, it was the policy of the airline.

[6]See Titus 1:6 and 1:7

Prologue

A missionary had been scheduled to speak on Sunday evening and that he did. At the end of the service, Pastor Bill Stewart[1] stepped to the pulpit and announced, "I hereby resign as pastor of this church effective immediately. The reasons are personal." Pastor Stewart thence walked off the platform and out the door, leaving a stunned congregation and a shocked missionary speaker. The next morning, he came back to the church building and cleaned out his office, never again to darken the door of that church.

Stunned silence hovered in the church auditorium, broken only by sobs. The church had loved their talented young pastor. The people slowly departed to the parking lot, asking the church officers, "What's going on?" The officers did not know.

Pastor Stewart had attended and graduated from a well-known fundamental Baptist college in the mid-south during the 1970s. Upon graduating from college, he was honored when the pastor of his home church in the Midwest asked him to return and become the assistant pastor of the church. That he did. Not long thereafter, the senior pastor was strickened with a life-threatening disease and "Bill" as he was known to the congregation began to fill the pulpit. Shortly thereafter, the senior pastor died.

The church in due season called Bill Stewart to be the pastor of the church. He did so with the energy and enthusiasm of a young man. His preaching was passionate and his personality had a tinge of charisma. His beautiful young wife and children, together with him, were exemplary of a model Christian family. The church loved them. Furthermore, under his leadership, the church was growing and new members were being added regularly. The future looked bright for Pastor Stewart and his congregation.

Though the congregation had a significant proportion of grey hair, Pastor Stewart surrounded himself with younger couples and some of them became officers in the church. One day, a young deacon's wife called and asked if she could come and talk to the pastor at his office. Bill Stewart knew this woman well. She and her husband were close friends with him and his wife. The woman's name was Sherry Reinert.[2] She was young, vivacious, and skilled at displaying her femininity. Pastor Stewart, unwisely allowed himself to begin counseling the woman behind the closed door of his office.

Sherry would come at the appointed hour each week neatly and discreetly dressed with a slight fragrance of pleasant perfume about her. The pastor was surprised to hear her pour out her heart about an unhappy marriage. That was a shock to him. He had always assumed she and her husband were happily married. The counseling continued. As Sherry told of the ugly fights at home and the verbal abuse heaped upon her by her deacon husband, Bill Stewart at first was disgusted at his apparent two-faced deacon. Then when Sherry would begin to sob softly, Bill's emotions shifted from disgust of her husband to sympathy for her. He genuinely felt sorry for her. A bond of affection began to build.

Sherry was attractive and modest. She was not so much angry at her husband as hurt. Bill Stewart continued to empathize and sympathize with her. His heart went out to her. One day, when the time came for her to leave, Pastor

Stewart stood and walked around his desk alongside of Sherry. He put his arm around her shoulder and gave her a sympathetic hug. She hugged him in return, but her hug was more than just an arm around the shoulder. She fully embraced him and cried on his shoulder. Though he knew better, Pastor Stewart returned her full embrace. Something clicked. The chemistry was right. And Bill Stewart and Sherry Reinert proceeded to kiss each other – on the lips.

From that encounter, they began to meet surreptitiously. When Sherry's husband was away, she invited Pastor Stewart to her home for "counseling" – in the bedroom. On other occasions, Bill Stewart would invite her to his home (read – his bedroom) for further "counseling" when his wife and kids were gone. Ironically, this adulterous couple was getting away with it. Nobody suspected a thing, not the least the wronged spouses.

However, Pastor's Stewart's conscience was convicted and he was miserable. He knew what he was doing was wrong. Finally, he rose that night after the evening service and announced his resignation. He never did openly confess his sin. But little by little, the sordid mess became known as it inevitably does. His testimony of Christ was shot. His reputation was gone. Though his wife was willing to seek counsel, eventually their marriage fell apart. The kids were deeply wounded. His mother, a member of the church, was deeply hurt and embarrassed. His calling of God was ruined. His livelihood and chosen "profession" were over.

Not only was he an adulterer, he was just plain dumb. Ironically, the woman with whom he had the adulterous affair not long thereafter divorced her husband, but Bill and Sherry went their separate ways. The church was deeply wounded and its momentum came to a screeching halt. The Holy Spirit was grieved and the evil one sat and laughed. Such is a sad episode of moral failure in a church in modern

America. What is even sadder is that this sort of thing goes on with sickening regularity across the land.

* * * * *

Pastor Don Wilson[3] had graduated from a well-known Christian university and then had graduated from an established fundamental Baptist seminary. Over the next twenty years, he was a pastor of several churches on the east coast. His wife was attractive and they had three handsome children. His final pastorate was of a solid, well-established fundamental Baptist church in the mid-Atlantic region.

Pastor Wilson prided himself upon being a good administrator. He kept the church in the black financially. He kept the church staff on the up and up. He had a good reputation in the community and the people of the church generally liked their pastor. Moreover, under his leadership, the church had been able to do considerable remodeling of the church facilities. He was proud of the improvements. Pastor Wilson also prided himself on having a modern computer network installed in the church and Christian school offices.

One Friday afternoon, the day was slow as it sometimes is in any office. His sermons for Sunday were complete. His Sunday School lesson was prepared. The bulletins for Sunday were done. There was no one from the church in the hospital to visit. Most of the staff had gone home for the weekend and he had nothing to do at home that he could think of. His office door was shut.

The thought occurred to Pastor Wilson that if he was going to preach against sin, he needed to know what he was talking about. He was aware of pornography on the internet, but had never really sought it out. Therefore, he reasoned, maybe I should find out how easy it is to find pornography on the web and see what it is all about. Then, I can be better prepared to warn our youth about it.

And so, he pulled up a standard internet search engine. He typed in several sex-related words, and immediately, a plethora of websites were listed. Partially in curiosity and part out of prurient desire, he clicked on several sites. On his screen, up came hardcore pornography.

Well, Pastor Wilson had learned how easy it was to find pornography on the internet. And, from the lewd and lascivious nature of the pictures, he surely could have preached against it. That should have been the end of it. But then the lust of the flesh took over and Pastor Wilson began to click on other sites and filled his eyes with many pornographic pictures. He typed other words into the search engine and found even more sexually explicit sites. He eventually was convicted of his sin and logged off the internet.

However the next week, he could not resist the temptation to look up other lurid websites and did so in the privacy of his office. It soon became an addictive habit. Before long, Pastor Wilson figured out how to copy lurid pictures from pornographic websites and then store them on his computer. Furthermore, he used his credit card to subscribe to sexually explicit websites.

What the pastor forgot was that his office computer was on a network of other computers. A man in the church volunteered his time to maintain the church system. One evening while doing routine maintenance, this good man stumbled onto files on the office server of which he was suspicious. He opened them and was shocked to find pornography on the church computer system. He was even more shocked to track the files back to the pastor's office computer.

In the course of events, the deacons of the church were notified. A meeting was called and the pastor was confronted with the evidence. He admitted his guilt. That Sunday morning, he announced his resignation. Not only was he guilty, he had been industrial-strength stupid. His poor wife was humiliated. His children were stunned. His ministry was over. He was without an income. He was forced to quickly move from the church parsonage and find other housing. His reputation was ruined. His peers were shocked. And worst of all, the testimony of Christ was besmirched. Again, the devil sat and laughed.

Was this an isolated event? Sadly no. It is happening all across the land. What a tragedy and travesty of the grace of God!

* * * * *

Tim Johnson[4] had had a golden baritone voice since he was in high school. People sighed and said "amen" when he sang. He went off to a well-known Christian college and there was further trained in voice, music, and church ministries. After graduation, Tim served in a number of churches as choir director and song leader. He was a nice guy – likeable. Though very talented, he did not have the inflated ego which some talented musicians have. He was easy to work with as well.

Eventually, Tim took a position with a large church in a city in mid-America. He and his family moved to begin his new ministry. There, among other things, Tim directed the well-established church choir. They had regularly scheduled rehearsals on Thursday evenings which went for several hours each week.

Tim was well liked by the choir and they responded to his gentle leadership. In the second row of the alto section sat Linda.[5] She was a dark-haired beauty with an equally beautiful voice. Tim, in due season, asked her to sing with him in a mixed trio. This meant more rehearsal time.

Tim's marriage was fair. There were no open problems, but the honeymoon had been over for a long time. Furthermore, he was away from home much of the time. His relationship with his wife became somewhat distant. Linda the alto, however, was vivacious, perky, and spent a lot of time with Tim at various rehearsals. This turned into having coffee together from time to time. Tim knew he was becoming emotionally involved with his pretty songmate. Their friendship soon turned to caresses and then kisses and then adultery altogether.

As things of this nature are hard to keep under a bushel, the dirty secret of Tim and Linda became known. He was fired. He left his wife and family and moved in with Linda, eventually marrying her after his divorce went through.

What a sordid mess! Their testimony as born-again Christians was besmirched. His wife and children were shell shocked. His ministry was over. His income had evaporated. His godly parents and extended family were crushed. The church was shaken and the devil once again sat and laughed.

The Problem

The problem is moral failure in God's people, particularly those in places of leadership. At the time of this writing, I have been in the gospel ministry for approximately 37 years. It seems the problem is epidemic. Though such tragic and sordid stories have certainly existed in years of yore, the frequency today is appalling.

Our Lord spoke of the wicked and adulterous generation which existed in his day.[6] If that were true then, it is at least as bad today – probably worse. We live in a day where the common morals of western culture and society have degenerated to an all-time low.

In one of the sordid stories mention above, I had the occasion to counsel some of the parties in the aftermath of that particular adulterous affair. As it turned out, the "other woman" heard that my wife and I were counseling the broken-hearted innocent wife. She therefore asked for an appointment. The inspired scriptural penman of Proverbs 30 marveled at the self-righteousness of adulterous women.

> "*There be three things which are too wonderful for me, yea, four which I know not: The way of an eagle in the air; the way of a serpent upon a rock; the way of a ship in the midst of the sea; and the way of a man with a maid. Such is the way of an adulterous woman; she eateth, and wipeth her mouth, and saith, I have done no wickedness*" (Proverbs 30:18-20).

Some adulterous women have no remorse or guilt of conscience. Such was the guilty party who came to my office one day. Her attitude was that she had not really done anything wrong. She had just met the "needs" of her illicit lover and he hers.

There seems to be little difference between various church groups or denominations. There surely is an inclination in a given group or fellowship to think that such moral failure is a problem in other circles – especially of rival fellowships. And then, the sad and bitter story arrives of a leader who has fallen in one's own circle. The entire nation has heard of the sordid debacles of Jim Bakker, Jimmy Swaggart, and Ted Haggard. The temptation is to self-righteously moralize and conclude that such are the proclivities of the charismatics. And then the bitter and sordid news of a preacher close to home bubbles to the surface. And the truth is, that in virtually every fellowship, association, or group; similar tragic failures have taken place. The national media or even the Christian media may not pick up on them. But in state after state and city after city, Bible-believing, born-again – and in many cases – fundamental Baptist leaders have and are falling into moral failure. The attrition rate is disgraceful

Three Categories of Failure

Though sin is sin and moral failure in the ministry is moral failure, it has been the observation of this writer, there seems to be three categories of fallen leaders. As will be noted, there is a progression of wickedness.

Good Men who Succumb to Temptation

The tragic thing in some of these failures is that the fallen leader has otherwise not really been an immoral man. And by that, I mean, he has not had a track record of such. His life has been exemplary and he has been faithful to his wife and his Lord. But then one day – one day – the tempter succeeded in laying a trap for him. The traps are often there. Many overcome the temptation. (We will explain the how and why in a later section.) But one day, a man yields to temptation.

I am convinced that Satan uses members of the opposite sex to seek to destroy those in positions of spiritual leadership. It is one of his devices.[7] But nevertheless, it only takes once for an individual to fail morally. When in places of spiritual leadership, "*unto whomsoever much is given, of him shall be much required: and to whom men have committed much, of him they will ask the more*" (Luke 12:48). Ordinary people in the world dabble in sexual sin all the time. But when one in Christian leadership does so, it is altogether another matter. For a pastor or one in the ministry, it disqualifies him from serving. He no longer is blameless.[8]

Accordingly, the devil seeks to lay traps for God's servants. It is one major way of damaging God's work. In my own ministry, there have been several occasions over the years, which I believe in hindsight, were just such traps. By the grace of God and the principles which will be laid out later in this book, this preacher did not succumb to the temptation.

In the early years of my ministry, I taught a young-adult-couples' Sunday School class. In those years, it was my custom to go out on Saturday morning and make brief visits for the class. I called them 60 second calls. I usually would stop at a door and knock. When the member of the class appeared at the door, I would say "Hi, how are you today. I sure hope to see you in our class in the morning. I'll be looking for you. See you tomorrow." Rarely did I enter a home. By keeping it short and sweet, I could visit quite a few homes in a two hour period on Saturday morning.

As a result, our class grew to a substantial size. I certainly did not visit the same people every week. But the 60 or so young adults in my class came to know that their Sunday School teacher very well might knock on their door on Saturday morning.

One young couple, the Pierces[9], came to Sunday School or church services sporadically. But we were trying to win them altogether. Others of their greater family either attended or had joined the church. So I would stop by their place briefly on a fairly regular basis. Sally Pierce[10] was a strikingly attractive woman. Her husband Ted was a nice guy. But at the time, I did not know they were having marriage problems.

Anyway, one summer Saturday morning, I stopped, hoping to catch both of them home. Unbeknownst to me, Ted had to work that day. However, Sally knew there was a chance I might stop by and she was waiting. When I rang the door bell, she evidently had looked out the window and saw my car in the driveway. When she opened the door, she was dressed immodestly to put it mildly. She feigned, "Oh, I didn't know anyone was at the door. Ted's working" Then she purred very pleasantly, "But come on in."

I was embarrassed by her brazen scheme and blurted out, "I've got to go." With that, I turned on my heel and departed post haste. As I got into my car, the phrase "the answer is NO" rang through my mind.

Satan had laid a trap. To me, Sally was a very attractive woman even when properly clothed. It was apparent she had adulterous intentions. She was home alone. I was there alone at her doorstep. She appeared at the door partially undressed. I easily could have slipped into the house and become history. By the grace of God and the principles to be laid out later in this book, I did not. Sadly, other good men have succumbed when Satan laid an attractive trap before them.

* * * * *

Years later, an attractive professional woman and her husband began attending our church. Their names were Jackie and Russ Thomas.[11] In the course of events, Jackie divorced Russ. Time passed and she was involved with at least one other man. Neither she nor her ex-husband attended our church any longer. In the meantime Jackie had cosmetic surgery to "augment" her anatomy.

One bright summer day, many in the church had been invited to a wedding and the reception afterwards. As the pastor, my wife and I of course were present. To my surprise, Jackie showed up for the reception. Knowing what I did, I really did not want to talk to her. I therefore only made a perfunctory greeting when we passed. However, to my surprise, she seemed inordinately friendly. It was like she had just met a long-lost friend. Moreover, her body language transmitted a message that bordered on flirtatious.

I went through the food line with my wife. She was detained by another acquaintance, so I found an empty table and sat down with my plate of refreshments. Moments later, Jackie walked up and stopped across the table from me. She asked if she could sit down. (She was wearing a moderately low-cut top.) She then bent over to place her plate in such a way that this preacher had a full view of her augmented anatomy. It was no accident. She did so intentionally. As I quickly perceived this woman's actions and body language, the message became evident. She was clearly saying in a non-verbal way, "If you are interested, I am willing." I gathered my wits and said, "Oh, I see my wife over there." I got up, food and all, and left. In my mind echoed the refrain, "The answer is 'NO!'"

There is no question in my mind that this woman was on the prowl. I evidently had looked like a good prospect that day so she plied her wiles on me. She was attractive. She was shapely. She was available. And, she signaled she was willing. It would have been very easy to make an appointment for a visit several days later and this preacher would have become another notorious statistic. By the grace of God and the principles to be found later in this book, I did not!

Thus, the devil seeks to lay traps for the unwary. Many escape the trap. Yet, some otherwise heretofore moral individuals succumb to the temptation. For others, the sin is more than a one-time yielding to temptation.

* * * * *

Sin Takes Root

Though some spiritual leaders fall into sin once, others continue therein after having fallen. The devil comes and suggests, "Well, if you have gone this far, you might as well keep on." Of course, the devil never calls it sin. He will freely provide all manner of excuses and rationalizations why moral failure really is not so bad after all. For example, the devil suggest, "I am meeting her needs." Or, "she is meeting my needs," etc. But the conscience is deadened and the sin becomes a sinful habit.

Other stories could be told of those who figured out a way to justify their sin and then just continued to repeat the wickedness – sometimes at length. Whether the sin is ongoing adultery, developing a taste and habit of pornography, or some other lascivious activity; for some, their sin becomes far more than having yielded to temptation once.

Bill Jones[12] was an unsaved young man in the Northeast who dated a girl in his last year of high school and continued to do so after they graduated. During that time they had sex on a number of occasions. Eventually, they went their own ways. Bill went in the military. She stayed in her home area.

While in the armed forces, Bill heard the gospel and got saved. He began to grow in the Lord and in due season felt God's call upon him for full-time Christian service. Upon being discharged from the service, he enrolled at a well-known Bible college and began to prepare for the ministry. During that time, he married and began a family. Upon graduation, Bill determined to return to his home area and plant a new church. He thus launched out with the blessing and assistance of the group of churches whence he was schooled.

Bill was able to get the new church off the ground and it was slowly developing. However, to support his family, he had to work on the side in a part-time secular job. One day while working, he ran across the girl he had dated in high school. The old flame began to flicker again. They met surreptitiously and soon took up where they had left off a decade earlier. What had been fornication then was now adultery. They got away with it. Nobody knew. Though he was initially convicted of his sin, his old flame was a hot item and his lust for her remained. Thus, they continued in their sin. It was bad enough that Pastor Jones had yielded to the temptation to commit adultery. But now he rationalized, what difference does it make. He was guilty, so why not enjoy it. Their secret rendezvouses continued for months.

However, the day inevitably came when they were caught. Someone from the church saw them together. Bill Jones resigned as pastor. His wife left him and eventually their marriage fell apart. The young church he had so diligently worked to establish collapsed. His testimony was ruined. His ministry was shot. His training for the ministry was wasted. A young man who had set out to serve God became a castaway. And, once again, the devil sat and laughed.

A Seared Conscience

Worst of all are those who hide their sin year after year. They become hypocrites of the worst sort. Though they might stand and preach righteousness, the reality of the matter is that they themselves are whoremongers or addicted to some form of lasciviousness. Their sin is cleverly covered – for a long time. But inevitably, such sin floats to the surface. Sin of a moral nature rarely is hidden forever. It eventually becomes known.

* * * * *

Dan Pattison[13] grew up in a Christian home. His father was a pastor and he accordingly was a regular church attender. However, in high school he ran around with loose girls and committed fornication with at least one of them. A pattern of life began. Nevertheless, Dan attended a good fundamental Christian college. Yet, on at least one occasion during summer breaks, Dan used the services of a prostitute. He seemingly repented thereof and went on.

Dan graduated from college and went on to seminary. There he married and started a family. He eventually became a pastor on the West Coast. Yet, the pattern of immorality earlier in life made him an easy target for the tempter. Like a reformed alcoholic, finding it is easy to start drinking again, the devil found it easy to tempt Pastor Dan.

One warm day, while driving down the street of a seedy part of town, Dan saw what appeared to be a prostitute standing on the corner. She was provocatively dressed and beckoned him to her. Men of stronger morals would have departed quickly. Yet, Dan had been there and done that before. The inhibition which a more upright man might experience had already been lowered by Dan's earlier acts of immorality. So he pulled his car over, lowered the window, and began to negotiate with the harlot. To his horror, he was suddenly arrested. The prostitute turned out to be a female undercover police officer. She was working as a vice sting operation. Other officers were hidden nearby and as soon as the decoy officer gave the signal, they swooped in for the arrest.

The news media quickly learned that a "fundamental" Baptist pastor had been arrested for soliciting a prostitute and proclaimed the sordid news. Pastor Dan's lame excuse was that he was simply curious to see what "that kind of woman" would say. Because his crime was a misdemeanor, he was slapped on the wrist with a small fine. Pastor Dan managed to convince his deacons and congregation that this was a one-time foolish act and begged their forgiveness. They forgave him. However, a cloud now hung over his ministry. Not long thereafter, he resigned that church and went elsewhere.

Sadly, his wife later told me of liaisons her adulterous husband had had with other women as time passed. She discovered pornography on his computer. Then she discovered phone numbers of other women in his cell phone and calls from them on his voice mail. It seems Dan had gotten involved with online "escorts" and met with the likes whenever he could sneak away. The last straw was when he was caught in the act with a woman at a public park one evening. Dan Pattison had literally become a whoremonger. His conscience was seared. His track record of sexual immorality, which began in high school, followed him through life.

His testimony was utterly besmirched. He resigned his church, quit the ministry, and left his wife. His family was both disgusted and heart broken. And the devil sat and laughed. Such is the ignoble end of a spiritual leader who allowed his conscience to be seared.

* * * * *

Jerry Wagner[14] once was one of the rising stars within independent Baptists. His famous father appointed him as youth pastor of the large church of which he was pastor. Accordingly, Jerry Wagner built a large and powerful program. Even before he graduated from college, Jerry Wagner had been awarded an honorary doctorate. His family name brought instant recognition anywhere in independent Baptist circles. He was dynamic, handsome, and carried an air of charisma about him. He was a powerful young preacher and had a following in his own right.

Yet, Jerry Wagner had a dark side. Though unknown at the time, even as youth pastor, he had committed fornication with girls in his own youth group. He picked the pretty ones and managed to seduce some of them. It was not a one-time episode. He also committed fornication with young ladies at the Christian college with which he was associated. Still a young man, this fellow had a seared conscience. After getting married, his fornication became adultery as he continued to hit on whatever pretty young woman he could seduce. When he later became the senior pastor of his own church, the adultery continued. He had managed to hide it from his wife and the church, but before long it would explode in his face.

One day, his wife happened onto nude pictures Jerry had taken of some of the women with whom he had been involved. At the same time, the deacons of the church became independently aware of the sordid mess as well. Jerry's ministry was over and his marriage soon fell apart. The rest is history. He had smeared filth across the name of Christ. He had severely damaged two churches. He had deeply wounded his faithful wife. His ministry and reputation were shot.

Though the devil laughed, this man's sin was the result of years of a seared conscience. He was a fornicator, adulterer, and whoremonger. His moral failure was catastrophic. As a teenager he had surrendered his purity and established a precedent in his life which haunted him for years thereafter. Because he had a long track record of immoral sexual liaisons with females willing to accommodate him, there were no inhibitions, modesty, or morality which hindered him the next time the lust of his flesh took an interest in another female. He had a seared conscience.

* * * * *

The bottom line is that moral failure renders a man no longer blameless and hence disqualifies him from the gospel ministry. Yet, as described above, there certainly are degrees of failure. For some, it was a one-time fall into adultery or impurity. For others, such sin became a habit after the initial fall. Yet for others, a lifetime of immorality utterly seared their conscience to the degree they no longer had any shame. But in every situation, moral failure ruined a ministry and damaged the testimony of Christ and His work. One can only imagine the day when they stand before Christ and give an account to the Chief Shepherd. I surely have no desire to be in their shoes.

Chapter Notes

[1]This is a fictitious name as will be all names given in this book. The event described is true. However, I have changed the names of the parties and distorted a few details to obscure identification of the real people and churches involved.

[2]Again, this is a fictitious name.

[3]Again, this is a fictitious name.

[4]Once again, this is a fictitious name.

[5]Again, a fictitious name.

[6]Matthew 16:4

[7]See II Corinthians 2:11

[8]I Timothy 3:2

[9]A fictitious name.

[10]Not her real name.

[11]Once again, these are fictitious names.

[12]Again, a fictitious name.

[13]Once again, a fictitious name.

[14]Once again, a fictitious name.

Section One – The Cause of Moral Failure

Chapter 1
Personal Testimony

By the grace of God, this author has maintained moral fidelity. I was a virgin when I married at the age of 24. I was not intimate with anyone prior to marrying my wonderful wife. I say that not to brag, for it is only by the grace of God. The benefit of such discretion, however, is manifold. Not only was I morally pure as I began the ministry, I was not encumbered by sexual "experiences" through fornication with other females. There was no precedence. On my wedding night, sexual intimacy was an altogether new experience. The point is it would have been awkward for me to engage in fornication, even if I had wanted to. There is a moral inhibition in virginity.

I well remember an incident while in seminary before I married my wonderful wife. That particular year, I lived in an apartment building that was in a deteriorating neighborhood. The building was owned by the seminary and housed only seminary students. The house across the street however had several apartments and housed people of the world. The church in which the seminary was located owned the old house across the street. It was slated for demolition to make way for a coming addition to the church.

One soft autumn afternoon, I was standing outside my building when from across the street came a siren call from a young-adult female hanging out an upper window. She was dressed less than modestly and invited me, a complete stranger, to come up and visit her. I don't know if she was a prostitute or just a loose young woman who thought this seminarian was attractive. Her motives, in any event, seemed less than pure. I can honestly say I was repulsed by the thought. Moreover, the next day, I contacted the man in the church who managed that property and reported the behavior of the tenant. He not long thereafter evicted her from the building.

The virginity I had maintained throughout high school, college, and then seminary became a shield of protection. To be honest, I wouldn't have known what to do with such a woman. Furthermore, the prospect of meeting with a woman of loose morals was abhorrent to me.

Not long thereafter, I married my wife. With God as my witness, I can honestly say that I have not had sexual intimacy with any other woman in my life. Nevertheless, I consider myself a red-blooded man. I find the opposite sex attractive. I often must force my eyes away from gazing on immodestly dress females in the world. I think that I probably have as much sexual desire as any other normal male. Over the years, pornography has inadvertently passed in front of my eyes on occasion and the lust of my flesh wants to look. But I have not allowed such desires to be fulfilled.

Am I some kind of super Christian who has never been tempted? The answer certainly is no. I have faced temptation of various kinds over the years as noted already in this book. But by the grace of God, I have not succumbed thereto.

The reason is basic spiritual principles and practices have controlled my life since not long after I was saved in 1966. Those spiritual principles are what this book is about. They are simple. But they are profound in their simplicity. I believe that the moral fidelity which God has enabled me to maintain can be achieved by any and all of God's people. That which follows will describe those principles.

I do not consider myself an expert in this area. I have not done any "studies" of social behaviors. I am not a psychologist or "therapist." But I know the principles and practices which have kept this preacher from the moral failure which is so prevalent in this wicked and adulterous generation. In the chapters to follow, I will share them with you the reader. Do not take any of this lightly for I believe the scriptural principles and practices about to be presented are a whole. Applying only bits and pieces of the coming advice is tantamount to putting on only parts of protective armor.

Though the principles to be presented are not exactly the classic armor of God described in Ephesians 6:11 and following, the advice of the Apostle at this juncture remains, "*Wherefore take unto you the* <u>*whole*</u> *armour of God*" (Ephesians 6:13). The people of God need *all* of the protective principles about to be set forth. Like a suit of armor, put on the whole works. To do less, very well may enable the evil one to find a gap in that armor whereby he may inflict damage between the joints thereof.

The principles to follow are eminently scriptural and practical. Moreover, they are profound in their simplicity. So, let's proceed to examine them.

Chapter 2
The Works of the Flesh are Manifest

The Apostle Paul wrote the inspired words, "*Now the works of the flesh are manifest, which are these; Adultery, fornication, uncleanness, lasciviousness*" (Galatians 5:19). He proceeded to also list another thirteen works of the flesh in the following two verses. For a born-again Christian, understanding the flesh and its counterpart the spirit is important in understanding moral failure. This is true whether the guilty party be one in spiritual leadership or anyone else for that matter.

The fact of the matter is, *all* sin and particularly *all* sexual sin are works of the flesh. It emanates from the sinful human nature which each and every one of us possess. The sinful nature you and I have can be traced back, both spiritually as well as seminally, to Adam. When he, in rebellion and disobedience to God, sinned; his human nature fell. It became distorted. The human spirit in Adam and Eve no longer was holy and pure. It had been sullied by the deceitfulness of sin. That fallen, depraved, sinful nature is called the flesh in the New Testament. It refers not so much to our physical flesh as to our inherent spiritual nature. From the sinful old flesh can develop any of the seventeen ugly "works" listed in Galatians 5:19-21.[1]

The first four works of the flesh listed are all sexual in nature. They all are forms of moral impropriety. Let's look at them in reverse sequence.

Lasciviousness is translated from the Greek word ασελγεια (*aselgeia*). It refers to unbridled lust or lewd thinking. This is where moral failure begins for anyone. Impure thoughts, lustful thoughts, sexual fantasies all fall under this description. It is impure thinking. The world is full of it with dirty jokes, suggestive themes in entertainment, clothing designed to stimulate sexual lust, and endless other forms of suggestiveness. It is all around us all the time. In Ephesians 4:19, the Apostle describes the mentality of most people in the world: "*who being past feeling have given themselves over unto lasciviousness.*" The world is a cesspool of filthy thinking – thoughts of lust, fornication, adultery and endless lewd acts. Moral failure begins with impure thinking. "*For as he thinketh in his heart, so is he*" (Proverbs 23:7). Sow a thought, reap an act. Sow an act, reap a habit. Sow a habit, reap a character. Sow a character, reap a destiny. Therefore, we must bring into captivity every *thought* to obedience to Christ.[2] Moral failure begins with impure thoughts.

From lasciviousness develops the next step – *uncleanness*. The word so translated is ακαθαρσια (*akatharsia*). From an unclean mind develops such unclean matters as pornography. It is of interest that the concept of pornography literally means "dirty literature." The Greek word πορνη (*porne*) refers to a prostitute. The Greek word γραφη (*graphe*) is whence the English words *graph* and *graphic* derive and basically refers to writing or literature. Hence, pornography essentially refers to impure literature or *uncleanness*. In the world in which we live today, such uncleanness manifests in numerous ways from old-fashioned pornographic magazines, to strip joints, to internet pornography, to phone sex, to sex chat rooms online. There seems to be no end to the unclean variations which the devil thinks up to ensnare men and women into moral impurity.

From uncleanness comes the next declension of moral character – *fornication*. The word so translated πορνεια (*porneia*), as is apparent, is a derivative of πορνη (*porne*) or uncleanness. It refers to illicit sexual intercourse. In this context wherein adultery is mentioned next, fornication refers to illicit sexual intercourse between unmarried parties.[3] Whether it is contact with a prostitute or an unmarried couple sleeping together, fornication is sex outside of marriage. Sadly, the mores of contemporary culture think nothing of fornication. In fact, young adults who remain celibate are considered abnormal by this wicked and adulterous generation. But God's moral standards have not changed. God has ordained that sexual intimacy take place in one context and that is the marriage relationship, period. The world scoffs at that. Yet, the Bible says, "*whoremongers and adulterers God will judge*" (Hebrews 13:4).

What the world refuses to grasp is that God's moral laws are ultimately for our own benefit. Promiscuity, frequenting prostitutes, homosexuality – all of which fall under the definition of fornication – are destructive and harmful behaviors. Sexually transmitted diseases which left untreated can lead to death, not the least of which are syphilis and ultimately AIDS. Fornication deflates feelings of self-worth and leaves a guilt ridden conscience. Thus, fornication is debilitating emotionally. Deep are the scars and emotional wounds which often result from such behavior. And, of course, one of the most garden-variety consequences is unwanted and illegitimate pregnancies with all the negative consequences arising therefrom. God knows what is best. His counsel therefore is "*flee fornication*" (I Corinthians 6:18). That commandment is ultimately in our best interest.

Notwithstanding, the lust of the flesh is powerful. When lustful thoughts, augmented by pornography or other lewd enticements run their full course, fornication often takes place amongst unmarried parties in the world. And, the world is full of the ugly aftermath of such behavior.

However, the same impure and destructive lusts can develop for those who are married. It is called *adultery*. The Greek word is μοιχεα (*moicheia*) and simply means adultery. Adultery is far more destructive than simple fornication. Not only do the guilty parties engage in illicit sexual contact, there also is a breach of contract between each guilty party who is already married. Marriage is a covenant (i.e., a contract) between a man and woman. They pledge themselves to each other and only to each other. To commit adultery is a breach of that contract. It is not only immoral, it is dishonest and usually covered by numerous lies. It is the ultimate of moral failure. When a man in spiritual leadership gets into a bed of adultery with a woman, he no longer is blameless. And that is the first qualification for a pastor and by extension anyone else in spiritual leadership.[4]

However, what is even more basic is that any of these four foul works of the flesh are just that. Whether it be viewing pornography or engaging in adultery, these are works of the flesh, plain and simple. The basic cause of moral failure goes right back to walking in the flesh. There is no difference in this regard between a famous spiritual leader or an obscure pastor in Podunk Center. Each can either walk in the flesh or walk in the Spirit. When one walks in the flesh, he is capable of any of the first four categories of the works of the flesh: Adultery, fornication, uncleanness, or lasciviousness. It makes no difference if one has an earned doctorate, an honorary doctorate, or never graduated at all. The works of the flesh are universal. Therefore, the real issue is getting the victory over the flesh.

Because a man is a pastor (or occupies some other position of spiritual leadership) is no immunity to the lusts of the flesh. To the contrary, the devil very well may target such an one with temptations ordinary believers might not have to contend with.

Chapter Notes

[1]I am of the opinion that the thirteen sins listed in Galatians 5:19-21 are merely typical. There certainly are more than thirteen categories of sin. But Paul here lists sins typical of the flesh.

[2]II Corinthians 10:5.

[3]In its broader sense, fornication refers to sexual immorality of any kind.

[4]"A bishop then must be blameless" (I Timothy 3:2).

Chapter 3
The Flesh Versus the Spirit

It should be no secret to those who are saved that we have two spiritual natures within. We were born physically with an old sinful human nature which is generally called the "flesh" in the New Testament. However, when we were born again, God's Spirit created within us a new nature that is variously called the new man, the new nature, or simply the "spirit" – a new spiritual nature within.[1] Both of these spiritual natures are present within a born-again Christian at any given moment. And, a born-again Christian will live (i.e., walk) in either nature at any time.

The victory in the Christian life is disciplining ourselves to live in the new nature and not the old. It is not as easy as it might seem. But it is basic Christianity. Let's look more closely at the two natures within us and how they operate. It is crucial to understanding moral failure and preventing its occurrence in the future.

The Old Nature

When Adam and Eve chose to disobey God's commandment and rebel against His will, their spiritual natures fell. Human nature from that point onward became distorted, sinful, and rebellious against God. This event, of course, is referred to generically as "the fall." That sinful nature has passed to every descendant of Adam from that day to this. When I was born, I inherited that sinful nature from my parents going back to Adam. So did you. To that degree, we are all the same. There is no difference, for all have inherited a sinful human nature called the flesh.

Affections and Lusts

The Apostle Paul describes our sinful nature – the flesh – in Galatians 5:17-26 (amongst other places). In 5:24, the Apostle describes the two characteristics of the flesh: *"affections and lusts."* Let us consider the second term here first.

Perhaps the most common descriptive of our old human nature is the term *lust*. It is translated from the word επιθυμια (*epithumia*). The nuances of the word range from garden-variety "desires, wants, and likes" to utter lasciviousness. Our old nature therefore operates on the frequency of what I want, what I like, and what I desire. In the context of moral issues, the word *lust* certainly descends to sexual desires. Outside of marriage, such desires are impure and immoral.

Hence, for a man (born again or otherwise) to look with lust on a woman not his wife is sin.[2] To look with lust at pornography is sin. Moreover, what is important to realize is that our old nature – the flesh – has a natural propensity for such. It is typical for a woman to not understand the male proclivity for pornography. However, every man understands it. It is just beneath the surface. It is sinfully natural – the lust of the flesh. Every man has such desires, albeit wrong. It is part of the fallen sinful nature with us.

God has created men to have a natural interest in women sexually. However, God has also ordained that the fulfillment of those desires take place within the marriage relationship. This is true whether it be sexual thoughts, sexual desires, or sexual acts. Moral failure occurs when one in spiritual leadership allows the lust of his flesh to develop outside of the marriage relationship. Whether it is the lascivious lust of pornography or involvement with a woman not one's wife, the lust of the flesh is at the root of it all.

The Apostle also used another term in Galatians 5:24 to describe a second characteristic of the flesh – the *affections* thereof. The word so translated is παθεμα (*pathema*) and pertains to our *feelings*. It derives from the more basic word παθος (*pathos*).[3] This aspect of our old nature is not so much related to moral issues except to the degree when one's feelings toward another can have adulterous overtones.

Notwithstanding, how many a Christian runs around with hurt feelings or makes decisions based upon how he or she "felt" about something? How many a young or carnal Christian fails to do what they ought to do because they did not "feel" like it? Our affections largely refer to our emotions and feelings. As we find ourselves being swayed by our emotions, we should pause and consider which spiritual nature from whence they derive – the flesh.

The New Nature

When an individual receives Christ as their personal Savior, he is born again – born of the Spirit of God. Accordingly, God, through His Spirit, creates within each believer a new nature, a new man. That new nature is born from above. The Apostle Paul described this new nature in Ephesians 4:24. There, he described our new nature as having been created in "*righteousness and true holiness.*" Thus, our new spiritual nature has two defining characteristics: righteousness and true holiness.

Righteousness and Holiness

In a coming chapter, we will delve into the matter of righteousness in considerable detail. Hence, we will not develop that concept at great length here. However, it is germane at this juncture to point out that righteousness is a radically different concept than "lusts" or "feelings." Whereas the old nature does what it does based on what it wants or feels like (whether legitimate or not), the new nature operates on a totally different frequency. The new nature does what it does based upon what is right or what it ought to do. That is vastly different than doing what one feels like or wants to do.

Likewise, the new nature has been created in "true holiness." This is the highest level of personal holiness. It is God oriented rather than self oriented. What a profound difference! Whereas the flesh operates on the level of doing what pleases itself and thus is self oriented, the new nature does what it does because it is pleasing to God and thus is God oriented. The one is self oriented and the other is others' oriented – namely God oriented. Therefore, one walking in the spirit will have a radically different attitude when temptation comes along.

One walking in the old nature will find pornography not only interesting, but will proceed on the basis of his desires or feelings aroused by a particular impure picture. However, one walking in the spirit, though finding a pornographic picture appealing naturally, will turn away because his orientation is toward pleasing God. Moreover, it is not right and therefore that settles it! He averts his eyes or removes himself from the place where such material is available.

Likewise, one walking in the flesh may find an attractive woman sexually interesting. He may at the least think lustful thoughts about the woman. If she communicates (whether verbally or otherwise) a willing attitude, the man walking in the flesh may decide to pursue the matter further. All things being equal, if the situation is conducive thereto, the man walking in the flesh may therefore engage in an act of fornication or adultery.

In contrast, though a man walking in the spirit may find the woman attractive, the prospect of adultery or fornication with her is abhorrent. It is not right and that settles it! Furthermore, his attitude is to please the Lord and fulfill His will. Therefore, though his flesh suggests she is attractive and maybe even willing, the answer is NO, period. Righteousness and true holiness have overruled the flesh and directed him to a totally different decision. Regardless of the attitude of the woman, walking in the spirit settles the matter. Once again, the answer is NO!! Case closed.

Put on the New Man

In Ephesians 4:24, the Apostle wrote these inspired words, "*And that ye put on the new man, which after God is created in righteousness and true holiness.*" We all have an old, carnal nature. If you breathe, you possess it. However, when we received Christ, God's Spirit created a new man – a new spirit – within us. Therefore, the Holy Spirit directs us to put on that new man. The analogy is of putting on clothing. Within the closet of our heart hangs the new lovely spiritual nature given to us by God when we were saved. The old dirty nature of the flesh is always present. Therefore, our duty is to put off the dirty clothing of the old nature and put on the new man each and every day. If, we fail to do so, the only other alternative is that we will walk in the flesh.

As a pastor, I from time to time remind our people of the necessity of continually putting on the new man. It would be easy if people could come forward at an altar call, kneel before God, and permanently put on the new man, once and for all, for the rest of their life. But God, in His infinite wisdom, has not so ordained such. Just as I need to put on clean clothing each day, so I need to put on the new man each day – sometimes more than once a day.

When I was a pastor in Florida, I would routinely take a shower each morning and put on clean clothing. However, in the afternoon, I might take some time to mow the grass under the hot Florida sun. In so doing, I would perspire not a little. When that chore was over, there often would be another shower and another change into clean clothes. And so it is in the Christian life. At a minimum, we need to put on the new man on a day-to-day basis. However, as temptation and the ugliness of the flesh manifests themselves, not only may there be occasion to confess sin during the day, but also the need to once again put on the new man.

It is the opinion of this writer that many, many born-again Christians – even those in positions of spiritual leadership – never pause to deal with the flesh and put on the new man on a regular basis. In my view, it is something which needs be done, at least, on a daily basis. Failure to do so, leaves only the alternative of walking in the flesh. And the works of the flesh are all unclean and bitter.

"Now the works of the flesh are manifest, which are these; Adultery, fornication, uncleanness, lasciviousness."[4] Once again, moral failure stems from one walking in the flesh. It is no more complicated than that. Therefore, in a word, the solution and prevention of moral failure is dealing

with the old nature and putting on the new man each and every day. We will go into this matter in considerable detail in a coming section.

The Flesh and the Spirit in the Pauline Epistles

Before moving on to other thoughts, let us pause and track in a bit more detail that which the Apostle Paul presented in the Pauline Epistles on this matter. There, the Apostle presented a consistent and frequent dealing with this important truth. In each case, the conflict between the flesh and the spirit is presented and in each case the Apostle directed us how to deal with the matter.

Romans 6:11-13

Though the Apostle does not mention the two natures by name in this passage, the twin parallels of sin and righteousness surely are present. "*Likewise reckon ye also yourselves to be dead indeed unto sin, but alive unto God through Jesus Christ our Lord.*"[5]

As will be discussed shortly, the New Testament clearly directs that we should crucify our flesh.[6] Here, the Holy Spirit directs us to reckon ourselves to be dead indeed unto sin. The word translated as *reckon* λογιζομαι (*logizomai*) is the same word found earlier in Romans and translated as "impute" or "account." In this context, it essentially has the idea to make up one's mind. The thought is of making up our mind to be dead to sin. This closely parallels the throught in Galatians 5:24 of crucifying the flesh. It is a decision which must be made. Furthermore, it is in the present tense indicating ongoing or continuous action. Hence, we find here an injunction from God to determine sin and our sinful nature as dead on an ongoing basis.

Then, we are directed to reckon ourselves alive unto God through Jesus Christ our Lord. Implicit in the matter of "reckoning" is that of making a decision – ahead of time. We need to make a decision each and every day, before the day begins, that we will be dead to the old nature and its concomitant sin. In its place, we must determine to live for Christ.

It is the firm view of this author that failure to do so leaves only one alternative – to walk in the flesh that day. And, the works of the flesh are manifest. An individual may not succumb to pornography or adultery immediately. However, walking in the flesh leaves the backdoor open for such temptation to enter.

Romans 7:15-25

In this familiar passage, the Apostle laments the struggle which even he had with his sinful old nature. If he battled with the flesh, how much more us?

> "*For that which I do I allow not: for what I would, that do I not; but what I hate, that do I. If then I do that which I would not, I consent unto the law that it is good. Now then it is no more I that do it, but sin that dwelleth in me. For I know that in me (that is, in my flesh,)dwelleth no good thing: for to will is present with me; but how to perform that which is good I find not. For the good that I would I do not: but the evil which I would not, that I do. Now if I do that I would not, it is no more I that do it, but sin that dwelleth in me. I find then a law, that, when I would do good, evil is present with me. For I delight in the*

> *law of God after the inward man: But I see another law in my members, warring against the law of my mind, and bringing me into captivity to the law of sin which is in my members. O wretched man that I am! who shall deliver me from the body of this death? I thank God through Jesus Christ our Lord. So then with the mind I myself serve the law of God; but with the flesh the law of sin.*"[7]

Once again, the Apostle Paul does not present the conflict directly as the flesh versus the spirit. Yet, the overall sense clearly is of that struggle. That of which he knew better, he did. And that which knew he should, he did not. He confessed that in his flesh was no good thing. Yet, the power to do as he ought seemed to elude him at times. The struggle so frustrated Paul that he referred to himself as a "wretched man." And yet, in the midst of that frustration and failure, the Apostle acknowledged the source of victory. That was through "Jesus Christ our Lord." Through the Spirit of Christ dwelling within and the new nature He has created, there is victory assured for God's people. It is walking in the spirit and not in the flesh. More on this soon.

I Corinthians 3:1-3

In Corinthians, the Apostle deals with the conflict between flesh and spirit more directly. "*And I, brethren, could not speak unto you as unto spiritual, but as unto carnal, even as unto babes in Christ. I have fed you with milk, and not with meat: for hitherto ye were not able to bear it, neither yet now are ye able. For ye are yet carnal: for whereas there is among you envying, and strife, and divisions, are ye not carnal, and walk as men?*

Though there certainly was sexual immorality in the Corinthian church, here the Apostle deals with a more garden-variety form of carnality: strife and division. Sadly when present amongst God's people, it emanates from the flesh. The Apostle draws the distinction between carnal Christians and those who are spiritual. In the greater context of the New Testament, I am of the opinion that which is addressed here as spiritual refers to those who walk in the spirit. And, indeed, a man walking in the spirit at that point is a spiritual man. Furthermore, such an one will not engage in the strife and bickering which was apparent in the Corinthian church. Such strife is typical of the works of the flesh catalogued in Galatians 5:20-21. The greater point is that when born-again Christians live, that is walk, in the flesh; any and all manner of sin typical of the old nature is possible. Hence, two distinct types of Christian living are denoted here: carnal and spiritual. There are no alternatives. It is an either or proposition.

II Corinthians 5:14-17

In this classic text, the Apostle sets forth once again the dichotomy between the two natures and the essence of the new.

> "*For the love of Christ constraineth us; because we thus judge, that if one died for all, then were all dead: And that he died for all, that they which live should not henceforth live unto themselves, but unto him which died for them, and rose again. Wherefore henceforth know we no man after the flesh: yea, though we have known Christ after the flesh, yet now henceforth know we him no more. Therefore if any*

> *man be in Christ, he is a new creature: old things are passed away; behold, all things are become new.*"

Not only are the two natures clearly hinted at, but the motive for walking in the new is set forth. That motive is love for Christ. It constrains or compels us to not live for ourselves (the old nature) but to live for Him who died for us (the new nature). He then concludes with a 'therefore' – "*therefore, if any man be in Christ, he is a new creature.*" God has made a new creature (or creation) within us spiritually. I can either live in the old nature or in the new. But one motive for walking in the spirit is my love for Christ. That, indeed ought to be a powerful motive for all believers. Sadly, it is not for some.

Ephesians 4:22-24

Moving past the clear teaching of Galatians 5, of which we will look at again soon, we come to Paul's admonition to the Ephesian church in this regard. There, he urged the Ephesian believers,

> "*That ye put off concerning the former conversation the old man, which is corrupt according to the deceitful lusts; And be renewed in the spirit of your mind; And that ye put on the new man, which after God is created in righteousness and true holiness.*"

The Apostle here clearly refers to the old nature as the "old man." He further notes how that former lifestyle was corrupt according to deceitful lusts. Once again, the *modus operandi* of the flesh is noted – deceitful lusts. Moreover, our old nature is corrupt. The word so translated is φθειρω (*phtheiro*) which also has the sense of depraved. As described earlier, the Apostle therefore enjoins God's people to put off the old nature and the lifestyle (i.e., conversation) derived therefrom. The analogy once again is of taking off dirty clothing. And then, as we typically do each day, to put on the clean clothing of the new nature – the new man. As noted earlier, that new nature has been created within us in righteousness and true holiness. Thus, whereas the old nature operates on the frequency of lust and fickle feelings, the new nature operates on the wavelength of doing what is right and pure before God. What a profound difference.

Colossians 3:8-10; 3:12

In a version similar to that which he wrote to the Ephesian church, the Apostle Paul wrote the Colossian church.

> "*But now ye also put off all these; anger, wrath, malice, blasphemy, filthy communication out of your mouth. Lie not one to another, seeing that ye have put off the old man with his deeds; And have put on the new man, which is renewed in knowledge after the image of him that created him.*"

And then in 3:12 he wrote, "*Put on therefore, as the elect of God, holy and beloved, bowels of mercies, kindness, humbleness of mind, meekness, longsuffering.*" In the context of putting off various sins (anger, wrath, malice, filthy speech, lying etc.), the Holy Spirit makes clear it is in the greater context of having put off the old man. Once again, the issue of the flesh is addressed. In a similar, though less direct thought, the inspired Apostle enjoined the Colossian church to put on kindness, humility, meekness, etc. Clearly implied is that these virtues are a result of putting on the new nature.

Summary

In summary, it is clear that in most of his epistles to churches, the inspired Apostle dealt repeatedly with the issue of the flesh versus the spirit – the old nature versus the new. From the old nature erupts all manner of sin and corruption, not the least of which is moral failure. The truth is, *all* sin in the life of a Christian flows out of the sewer pipe of the flesh. Likewise, the virtues of godliness, not to mention the fruit of the spirit develop from the new nature. Therefore, the real issue is a spiritual one.

Years ago, a simple truism was impressed upon my heart. That precept is that the issues of life are fundamentally spiritual. The issues of life – family, marriage, children, peace of heart, success in God's work, and fulfillment in life – are all spiritual in their roots. In like fashion, the negative issues of life – broken homes, divorce, wayward children, a troubled heart, failure in God's work, and frustration in life – likewise are also spiritual in their roots. The first group grows out of the new nature, the second from the flesh. Indeed, the issues of life are primarily spiritual. When a man crosses into moral failure, whether he is caught or not, the reason is spiritual. He is walking in the flesh.

* * * * *

Walk in the Spirit, and Ye shall Not Fulfill the lust of the Flesh

The above quotation is from Galatians 5:16. The essence of this book is summarized in that one simple, but profound, statement. The reason why men in spiritual leadership (or any Christian for that matter) descend into moral failure is that they are living in the flesh. That may sound trite, but it is at the center of the problem. God's solution is as simple as it is profound. If we would overcome the lust of the flesh, we must walk in the spirit.[8]

The grammar is instructive. When the Holy Spirit directed us to walk in the spirit, he promised *"and ye shall not fulfil the lust of the flesh."* The word translated as "fulfil" τελεσητε (*teleseite*) is conjugated in the aorist tense, active voice, and subjunctive mood. The latter is significant. The thought is that when we walk in the spirit, we *will not* fulfil the lust of the flesh. Among other things, the subjunctive mood refers to the human will. Again, when we walk in the spirit, we WILL NOT fulfil the lust of the flesh. Our spiritual heart is the seat of our will.

When the new nature – the spirit – is in control of our heart at a given hour, we will react to temptation in righteousness and true holiness. We will reckon ourselves to be dead indeed unto sin. The decision has already been made and that decision is simple. The answer is NO! We will not yield to the temptation. It is a promise of God! And, I can bear witness after many years that God keeps this promise.

The principle is so simple and yet so profound. As I have discussed this prospective book with others, external devices such as internet filters and accountability groups have been suggested. There is nothing wrong with either of those or other such preventive measures. But the issues of moral failure are internal and spiritual. Temptation will pop up when least expected and there are no external filters or sociological means to prevent such.

Witness David, who one evening happened to see Bathsheba bathing herself on her rooftop (or back yard). His palace was on the peak of a hilltop in east Jerusalem. Hers was at a lower elevation. David could look down upon any home on the hillside below his palace. Whether Bathsheba knew she would be visible to the king as she bathed herself is beside the point. David happened to see her and lust was conceived. The rest is history.

A preacher out visiting never knows when the devil will have a trap waiting for him. It may be an attractive prostitute on a street corner whose chemistry clicks with the preacher. It may be an attractive woman whose husband is not home when he knocks on their door. It may be unsolicited pornography that unexpectedly pops up or while on the road using a hotel computer. It may be emails which begin innocently, but descend into suggestiveness and then worse. The devil will always find ways to tempt.

A Christian man must have the internal spiritual ability to be ready to say NO! God's simple, yet powerful, solution to the lust of the flesh is to walk in the spirit – that is, to live in the new nature created in righteousness and true holiness. That is the universal spiritual prevention which any one can rely on at any time and under all circumstances. This issue in the Christian life is not a game. It is deadly serious. Lives, marriages, ministries, and reputations are all at stake. We today live in a society given to fornication and adultery. And, a man of God WILL be confronted with the temptation and opportunity to succumb thereto.

In the coming section of this book, we will explore in considerable detail the spiritual ingredients necessary to walk in the spirit. However, before delving into those principles, let me share with you a simple practice which I believe God has used to give me the ability to say, "The answer is NO" time and time again.

Seeking the Help of the Holy Spirit Each Day

In Galatians 5:24, the Holy Spirit moved the Apostle Paul to write, *"And they that are Christ's have crucified the flesh with the affections and lusts."* It is not my intention to overwhelm the reader with Greek minutia nor to seemingly correct the Bible. However, at times referring to the original language and nuances thereof are helpful in gaining understanding of a given verse. Without belaboring the grammatical structure, the thought could be rendered, "And they that are Christ's *crucify* the flesh . . . ." The verb tense is aorist and not perfect as the English translation might imply.

The idea is that we need to crucify the flesh as often as is necessary. I am of the opinion that this needs to be done at least once a day. This parallels the injunction in Romans 6:11 – to reckon ourselves to be dead indeed to sin. Crucifying the flesh is both a spiritual as well as a mental decision.

To crucify means to put to death. That is what Romans 6:11 deals with. In our mind, each day at the minimum, we need to put the old nature to death. It would be great if this could be done once and for all. Yet, that is not how God has ordained it.

In I Corinthians 15:31, the Apostle wrote, *"I die daily."* In all honesty, I believe he was referring to facing the prospects of dying a martyr's death on a day-by-day basis. That is the immediate context. However, I also believe that spiritually, this is exactly what we need to do each day. Crucify the flesh – to die thereto daily. As temptation arises throughout a given day and as we find ourselves wavering, we very well may need to crucify our flesh once again.

In the classic injunction of Romans 12:1, the Holy Spirit moved Paul to write, *"I beseech you therefore, brethren, by the mercies of God, that ye present your bodies a living sacrifice, holy, acceptable unto God, which is your reasonable service.*"

The word translated as "present" παριστημι (*paristemi*) also has the sense to "yield." And though the Apostle refers to our bodies here, that thought closely parallels the spiritual issue of the flesh – our old sinful nature. In essence, Paul directed to yield our flesh (i.e., our bodies) to God as a living spiritual sacrifice.

Therefore, tying this all together, *each* morning as I spend time with the Lord in prayer, among other things, I pray to this effect. "Holy Spirit of God, please help me to crucify my flesh this day. I yield myself to you. Please help me to walk in the spirit and not in the flesh this day." And with that simple prayer, I determine (i.e., reckon or consider) the flesh to be dead for that day. Does the flesh ever raise its ugly head during the course of the day? Unfortunately, yes. However, I then again seek the aide of the Holy Spirit in crucifying it once again. It is both a spiritual as well as a mental decision.

Once again, the alternative is to walk in the flesh that day. To not address the old nature will pretty well ensure that it takes the helm of my heart. And with the flesh at the helm that day, I will walk in the flesh and be prone to the temptations the evil one may throw before me that day.

Hence, the instruction of Galatians 5:16 remains profoundly important. *"This I say then, Walk in the Spirit, and ye shall not fulfil the lust of the flesh.*" It is the simple secret to victory in the Christian life. When we crucify our flesh and walk in the spirit on a day-by-day basis, we WILL NOT fulfil the lust of the flesh. The decision has already been made. When temptation arises, the answer is NO!

Simple isn't it? The following section will go into further detail on how to walk in the spirit.

Chapter Notes

[1]We shall focus in some detail in Galatians 5 where the Authorized Version routinely capitalizes the word *spirit* implying the Holy Spirit. See Galatians 5:16. However, it is the considered opinion of this writer that the word *spirit* in this context likely is not referring to the Holy Spirit. It is my view that the *spirit* here refers to the new nature created within us when we were born again. And, this spirit, of course, has been born of the Holy Spirit of God, so the point is almost moot. However, for insight into the concept being set forth by the Apostle, I am of the opinion that understanding the word *spirit* to refer to the new nature and not the Holy Spirit makes more sense and fits the context better. My reason for this conclusion is the clear parallel found here and elsewhere in the New Testament between the old nature and the new nature. That is the context here. As will be discussed shortly in this chapter, there is a clear pattern throughout the Pauline Epistles of the parallel and contrast between the old and new natures. That is the case in the latter portion of Galatians 5.

[2]Matthew 5:28

[3]The greater thought is how that our feelings stem from the old nature. This leads to our emotions which evidently have been distorted by the fallen nature as well. As will be developed later in this chapter, God has ordained for us to make decisions in life based upon what is right and not by how we "feel" about whatever. The greater thought here is of our emotions which are notoriously fickle. Of interest is Tchaikovsky's 6th Symphony entitled "*Pathetique*." It is a very emotion-evocative work with its powerful musical moods. Modern rock music does the same in a much more crude fashion. It appeals to one's emotions – our feelings.

[4]Galatians 5:19

[5]Romans 6:11

[6]Galatians 5:24

[7]Romans 7:15-25

[8]Once again as noted earlier in this chapter, this writer takes the view that the word *spirit* in the latter portion of Galatians 5 refers to our new spiritual nature in distinction to the Holy Spirit. As noted earlier, the original language did not present upper or lower case spelling to which we are accustomed. The capitalization of spirit in this portion is a matter of interpretation by the translators. As noted in the preceding section, there is widespread context for a contrast between the old and new natures in the Pauline Epistles. Hence, in discussing this issue, I will not capitalize spirit in this context.

Section II – How to Walk in the Spirit

Chapter 4
The Power of the Word

At the time of this writing, I have been saved for over forty years. Not long ago, while being driven from a major airport, I was asked by a younger preacher, "Dr. Sorenson, would you please tell me several books which have changed your life or ministry." As I thought on it, I replied, "Well, I can tell you of one Book that changed my life." And with that, I proceeded to share with that younger preacher how the Word of God changed my life and ministry.

As I look back over the past forty years, several men or messages made a profound influence on my life and they continue to influence me to this day. I will share them with you.

When I went to seminary in 1968, I sat for four years under the ministry of Dr. Richard V. Clearwaters who, even then, was the long-time pastor of the Fourth Baptist Church of Minneapolis, Minnesota. I later went on to become an assistant pastor under "Doc" as he was affectionately called. He was my pastor and mentor for four years.

Come January of 1969, Dr. Clearwaters, as he did every year, laid out a challenge for the church to read through the Bible, cover to cover, in the new year. He explained to us that by reading four chapters a day – three in the Old Testament and one in the New – that anyone could easily read through the Bible in one year. In Bible college, I had read the Bible through in one year as a requirement for the Bible Survey class all entering students were required to take. Apart from that, I had never made any effort to systematically read the Bible through. And so, in January 1969, I set out again to read the Bible through that year. To my recollection, I accomplished that goal. The concept of reading through the Word left an impression on me. However, in the succeeding years, I must confess that I backslid from that specific goal. I was in the Word daily, but not to the degree I that I was when under the discipline and goal of reading it through in one year.

Unfortunately, my personal Bible reading in those years became hit and miss and usually more miss than hit. Sadly, I think that is the situation of many a Christian, even for those in the ministry.

Psalm 1:1-3

In about 1972, my wife and I attended a seminar at McCormick Place in Chicago.[1] I suppose I was impressed as much by the architecture of McCormick Place as I was by any other aspect of that large gathering. However, one thing that was taught that week has stuck with me all these years. The speaker told how that as a high school student he had been an average-to-less-than-average student academically. He related how finally one day, he talked to his youth pastor about his grades. Whoever that man was, I do not know. However, the speaker related how his youth pastor took him to Psalm 1 and explained the importance of God's Word. In explaining Psalm 1 to him, the youth pastor pointed out the promise of God that if one would meditate in God's Word day and night, among other things, "*whatsoever he doeth shall prosper.*"[2] That promise therefore would include his grades.

The speaker then related how he began to spend time in God's Word each morning and night as directed in Psalm 1:1-3.

> "*Blessed is the man that walketh not in the counsel of the ungodly, nor standeth in the way of sinners, nor sitteth in the seat of the scornful. But his delight is in the law of the LORD; and in his law doth he meditate day and night. And he shall be like a tree planted by the rivers of water, that bringeth forth his fruit in his season; his leaf also shall not wither; and whatsoever he doeth shall prosper.*"

To his amazement, this young man's grades began to go up and he finished high school, as I recall, with an A minus average. He went on to college and continued the regimen of being in the Word day and night – starting each day and ending each day in the Word of God. However, in his second year of college, he had to go to work on the side to help pay his college bills. He concluded that he did not have time to do his regimen of Bible reading each morning and night. He therefore quit. Though he had had good grades his first year in college, to his dismay, he found himself struggling academically once again.

Then it dawned on him what had changed. He had turned away from the spiritual practice of being in the Word day and night as he had done for the previous several years. Though he was pressed for time, he once again returned to the regimen of going to the Word, literally, day and night. Once again, his grades began to rise.

The moral to that story is simple. God keeps His promises. In Psalm 1:2, the Holy Spirit described one who delighted in the Law of the Lord and meditated therein day and night. That might seem radical or extreme to some. However, God promised that for those who do, "whatsoever he doeth shall prosper."

Well, I am just simple enough to take God at His Word. If God said that meditating in His Word day and night would cause whatever I did to prosper, then I will go to the Word day and night. Once again, I began to read the Bible through once a year. That meant spending time in the Word in the morning and in the evening.

It has been my experience that many Christians go to the Word in the morning. However, I have not known many who do so both day and night. Yet, that is what God prescribed. When I was growing up in a Christian home, going to Bible camps and later to Bible college, there was constant talk about one having their "devotions" each day. By devotions, the idea was to read something out of the Bible and then pray.

There certainly have been a number of well-known "devotional" booklets. The format usually is a few verses, maybe a portion of a chapter in the Bible. That is followed by a paragraph or two of "devotional"thought. Well, as I began to read through the Bible day and night, the only place I found the word "devotions" was in Acts 17:23 and there it was in a pagan context.

The truth is, there is no place in the Bible which explicitly teaches God's people to have "devotions" each day. Implicit in that term is a bite-sized portion of Scripture, followed by a bite-sized prayer, and maybe a bite-sized commentary written by someone else. That thought is completely alien to the Scriptures. What I was reading in the Bible was about meditating day and night. David also wrote, "*O how love I thy law! it is my meditation <u>all the day</u>.*"[3] The Apostle

Paul wrote to the Colossians church, " *Let the word of Christ dwell in you richly.*"[4] The thought there is for the Word of Christ (i.e., the Bible) to dwell in our hearts abundantly, in large measure, in considerable quantity.

Joshua 1:8

When the Holy Spirit impressed upon David words of Psalm 1, David was actually commenting on instructions which God had given to Joshua in Joshua 1. There, God had directed Joshua:

> *"This book of the law shall not depart out of thy mouth; but thou shalt meditate therein day and night, that thou mayest observe to do according to all that is written therein: for then thou shalt make thy way prosperous, and then thou shalt have good success."*[5]

God's injunction to Joshua was clear. He was to meditate in the book of the Law – the Bible – day and night. Joshua had just been appointed as commander in chief over the infant nation of Israel. He would serve not only as a military commander, charged with conquest of the land, but also as the civil administrator and judge of the fledgling nation. It is hard enough to be the pastor of several hundred people. Imagine being the sole leader of two to three million people! God's simple strength and guidance for his new leader was to meditate in His Word day and night.

By that, God did not suggest that Joshua was to spend all his waking hours studying the Bible. Rather the thought is to think on the Word by day and by night (as is the literal reading in Hebrew). To meditate is to think on or reflect upon.

Yet, to think on the Word of God implies reading thereof in the first place. The simple thought, I believe, is that Joshua was to so fill his mind with the Word of God that he thought thereon throughout the day as he went about the burdensome tasks as the chief executive of the nation. Moreover, come night time, he was to do so then as well. I interpret that to mean that come eventide, God directed Joshua to spend time with or in His Word. At the very least, we can conclude that Joshua was directed to begin each day and end the day with his mind focused upon the Word of God. That comes down to spending time reading and then reflecting thereon each morning and evening.

Clearly implied is more than just a bite-sized snippet of Scripture. It is my view that God intended Joshua to saturate his mind with His Word. A significant portion of each twenty-four hour period was to be spent with and in the Word.

Then God said, "*that thou mayest observe to do according to all that is written therein.*" The purpose of going to the Word of God, day and night, was *so that* Joshua would observe to **do** according to **all** that was written therein. God's plan was simple. It was His purpose for Joshua to so absorb His Word to the degree he saturated his mind therewith. And the purpose for that was *so that* God's Word would begin to modify Joshua's behavior. And so it is to this day. When we saturate our minds with the Word of God, it will begin to modify our behavior. We will begin to do all that is written therein.

Here is why. As we saturate our minds with the Word, it will eventually soak down into our heart and influence the decisions made there. Our spiritual heart is the center of our being. It is the seat of the human will. It is where the decisions of life are made. In the Garden of Eden, Adam made a decision in his heart to disobey God. When David stood looking out from his hilltop palace and saw the immodest Bathsheba below, a decision was made in his heart to invite her to commit adultery with him. In contrast, Daniel purposed in his heart that he would not defile himself.[6]

When our mind is so saturated with the Word of God that it soaks down into our heart, the decisions we make will be profoundly influenced. Our behavior will be modified. As we shall shortly see, we *will* not sin against God. Furthermore, we will learn to do *all* of what God has directed us to do. The key is saturating our minds with the Word of God.

How many a Christian does *some* of what the Word of God commands? Certainly many of those who succumb to moral failure! They absorb enough of the Word to perhaps have right doctrine and observe many of God's precepts. However, they don't observe *all* of them. The reason is apparent. They have absorbed God's Word in a limited degree, but not altogether. Trouble lies ahead.

But then notice what God promised in this regard. "*For then thou shalt make thy way prosperous, and then thou shalt have good success.*" God promised Joshua that *if* he would meditate in His Word day and night, not only would he do all he was supposed to do, but *then* his way would prosper and *then* he would face good success. What a compounded blessing: prospering in the way and succeeding in the undertaking! God promised Joshua that the pathway of his life would prosper if he would meditate in His Word day and night. (That, by the way, is not my promise, but God's.) There certainly are pitfalls along the pathway of life. Losing one's ministry through moral failure certainly could be one of them. Rather, God promised a prosperous journey through life.

In similar fashion, God promised as Joshua filled His mind with His Word day, and night, that then he would have good success. In other words, he would succeed in whatever endeavor was set before him. What a promise! That is not to say that Joshua would become rich and famous. But God did promise that as he meditated on His Word day and night, year after year; his pathway through life would be prospered and he would succeed in his endeavor. That promise has never been abrogated. It remains in force to this hour. Sadly, most Christians, even those in leadership, ignore the condition for the promise – meditating day and night in the Word of God. It is at their own peril.

David went on to comment on God's promise to Joshua in Psalm 1:1-3. David's comment regarding one who meditated in the Word day and night is that *whatsoever* he did would prosper.[7] Whatever task, calling, ministry, or endeavor we undertake will prosper as we saturate our minds with God's Word to the degree it soaks down into our heart, modifying our behavior and directing our decisions.

* * * * *

About a year after attending the big seminar in Chicago, I had the opportunity to attend a much smaller conference being held at a church in Wisconsin.[8] The keynote speaker was a well-known preacher. I remember little about the contents of that conference. However, to this day I recall a challenge made then. The speaker challenged preachers in that conference to go home and make it a goal to read the Bible through seven times a year. It dovetailed with the conviction I was forming about being in the Word day and night.

The keynote speaker went on to describe how that by reading twenty-seven chapters a day, one could read the Word through seven times a year. He explained that because of the rigors of his ministry on the weekend, he usually only read eighteen chapters a day on Saturdays and Sundays. He went on to further describe that by breaking down the twenty-seven chapters a day into three segments – morning, noon, and night – the challenge became more realistic.

As I drove the 300 plus miles home from that conference, I decided, "If that preacher can do this, so can I." He likely was busier than I was and he managed to accomplish that goal. I had respect to him. At the time, he was an associate pastor of one of the largest churches in the world. Maybe his goal of reading the Word through seven times a day had something to do with his success in life. The words, *"And whatsoever he doeth shall prosper"* rang through my head. As I drove home, I began to outline in my mind how I was going to accomplish this task.

When I got home, the next day, I set out to achieve this goal. My initial plan was to read (as I recall) five chapters a day from the Pentateuch, four chapters a day in the history books of the Bible, three chapters a day in the poetry books, four chapters a day in the major prophets, two chapters a day in the minor prophets, three chapters a day in the Gospels, one chapter a day in either Acts or Revelation, three chapters a day in the Pauline Epistles, and two chapters a day in the General Epistles. I would read nine chapters each morning, nine over the noon hour, and another nine sometimes either around supper or before bedtime.

Well, after one week of that regimen, I paused and sighed, "This is going to be harder than I thought." It was taking a lot of time. But then, I determined that I would do it for at least one year and compelled myself to continue. That was more than thirty-three years ago. I have never stopped. Later, I streamlined my approach to simply read nine successive chapters straight through at a sitting. That is, if I was reading in Psalms, I would read twenty-seven chapters there in one day and so forth.

Over the years, the reading discipline certainly has become more overview reading, pausing to dwell on pertinent spiritual truths which were long ago underlined. It has not been in-depth reading. But it has conveyed several profound benefits. (1) I have been able to develop a solid grasp of the overall context of the entire Bible. And context is the major factor in hermeneutics – the science of interpretation. I believe that I understand the basic context of any given passage of Scripture as a result. (2) More importantly, maintaining the regimen of twenty-seven chapters a day, if nothing else, has literally kept me in the Word day and night for the past thirty-three years.

I can say without fear of contradiction that this practice has had a profound influence on my life. If for no other reason, this discipline has kept this preacher from moral failure. Such saturation of my mind with the Word of God has given strength to my new nature to overcome the lusts of the flesh. It has kept me walking in the spirit.

And so, as I sat in the car with a younger preacher as we drove from the airport, I told him the book which has influenced my life more than any other is the Word of God. Certainly, I have read other books. (I also have authored books.) But the saturation of my mind by the Word of God over these past thirty-three years is what has left a profound mark upon me. Whatever small success I have enjoyed, I believe, stems from this practice. To this degree, I believe that I have developed the mind of Christ.[9] It certainly has been a continual influence upon my heart and mind to say NO when the soft breezes of temptation have wafted by.

The Principle of Psalm 119:11

In the midst of the great one-hundred-nineteenth Psalm, the Holy Spirit moved David to write, *"Thy word have I hid in mine heart, that I might not sin against thee"* (Psalm

119:11). Conventional wisdom has routinely applied this verse to the memorization of Scripture. This author certainly is not opposed to memorizing portions of God's Word. However, in my view, Psalm 119:11 is used out of context in this regard. The rote memorization of Scripture is not what prevents one from sinning against God. Anecdotal evidence of that would be overwhelming. Rather, my understanding of Psalm 119:11 closely parallels what has been discussed above.

When one so saturates his mind with the Word of God that it soaks down into his heart, his decision making will be profoundly influenced. Here, David writes of our spiritual heart. He is not speaking of the cardiovascular organ pumping blood through our bodies. The sacred text here refers to our spiritual heart. Once again, our heart is the center of our being. It is the residence hall of our spirit. It is the seat of our will. It is the command center of our lives.

Even as a ship has a bridge from whence the captain commands the ship, so our heart directs our lives. Even as an aircraft has a cockpit from whence the pilot controls the plane, so our heart is where major decisions are made. Our heart is the seat of the will. It is where a decision to yield to temptation is made or where the answer NO is decided. When the Word of God soaks down into the heart from a mind saturated therewith, the human heart will not choose to sin against God. Conversely, when the heart is void of or has a low quotient of God's Word on hand, it may very well say "yes" when temptation calls.

The Hebrew grammar is instructive at this point. The thought translated "*might not sin*" is conjugated in the imperfect tense in the original text. One nuance of the Hebrew imperfect tense is similar to the subjunctive mood in Greek. That being said, the thought likely is this: "Thy Word have I hid in mine heart that I *will not* sin against thee." A heart where the Word of God has been absorbed in considerable degree *will not* sin against God. The will has been influenced. The heart, the seat of the will, has made a decision. It *will not* say yes to temptation. It *will not* sin against God. It *will not* succumb to the temptress' siren song or the lure of the pornographic image. The heart has been modified by the Word of God. It now will seek to observe to do all that is written therein.

The Word of God is powerful! However, it is the view of this writer that the weakness of modern Christians is the bite-sized absorption we have been led to think is acceptable. Only as we saturate our minds by going to the Word day and night (literally) will the Word of Christ dwell in us richly (i.e., abundantly). It is only when we saturate our minds with the Word that it will soak down into our hearts and influence our will. Then, the moral and spiritual strength develop to say NO to any moral or ethical temptation.

Sadly, many in Christianity today rather fill their minds with other things. It may be Christian radio. It might be Christian books. It might be reading or writing blogs on the internet. It might be listening to Christian music. None of these are wrong. But many have sacrificed the best on the altar of the good. Some of the examples of moral failure listed earlier in this book were men well-read in contemporary theological issues. Some were expert in the right kinds of Christian music. Some were leaders of institutions of education as well as being a preacher. Some were noted conference speakers.

But I strongly suspect that in each and every case of moral failure listed (or which could be listed), there was one common denominator. The guilty parties either never had or at least at the time of their fall were not in the Book day and night. Though their minds may have been filled with other decent things, they had not so saturated their minds with the

Word such that it soaked down into their hearts, modifying their will to say NO when the temptation came. The Word of God is powerful and will positively influence anyone away from sin.

The old saw was never more true. "This Book (i.e., the Word) will keep you from sin, but sin will keep you from this book." I have no idea who penned those words, but they are profoundly true. The Word of God, when absorbed in significant quantity and meditated thereon, will prevent sin. It is as simple as that.

* * * * *

I was recently astounded at a bit of information which came across my desk. As is the case with many preachers, I receive several regular email newsletters which are either theologically oriented or ministerially directed. One such newsletter is a compilation of theological and philosophical issues which comes four or five times a week. Sometimes it is just about world events or politics as they might pertain to a biblical viewpoint. This particular e-publication usually ends with a bit of humor. The editor routinely includes comments received from recipients of the newsletter, almost all of whom are pastors or spiritual leaders.

One day, not long ago, the editor sent out a comment from one of his readers to wit: "Dear Dr. so and so. Thanks for your insights and encouragement. I use your newsletter[10] each morning for my devotions." I was absolutely astonished. Whoever that respondent was, he had no reservations about admitting to a spiritual mentor that he had his "devotions" each day from an e-publication which was part theological, part philosophical, part current events, part political, and part humor. I have no idea who that fellow was.

He ostensibly was a fundamental Baptist pastor or spiritual leader somewhere or other.

It is bad enough when those in the ministry only ingest bite-sized portions of the Word each day. But here was a guy who openly admitted that his "devotions" were not even from the Word of God. No wonder there is moral failure in the ministry. Without the power of the Word of God in one's life, temptation will be all the more intense.

* * * * *

"*This I say then, Walk in the Spirit, and ye shall not fulfil the lust of the flesh*" (Galatians 5:16). We come full circle. Walking in the spirit will preclude fulfilling the lusts of the flesh. However, I know of no better way to walk in the spirit than by filling one's mind with the Word of God. The impetus and strength to walk in the spirit comes from the Word of God. It is what enables us to grow in grace. It is the spiritual milk, meat, bread, and water which nourishes the new nature. There is no substitute.

Most have heard the old parable about the white missionary working with the native American Indian convert years ago. As the story goes, the missionary had led the old Indian to Christ. Some years later, the missionary had the opportunity to speak with him again. The missionary asked the Indian how his Christian life was. The Indian reportedly answered, "Indian have black dog and white dog on inside. Black dog always fighting with white dog." To which the missionary asked, "Which dog wins?" The Indian replied, "Dog Indian feed most." And of course the application of that parable is that whichever spiritual nature we feed the most will be the stronger and will prevail. That parable has been used, no doubt, many times from countless pulpits across the land. It is usually directed at younger Christians. But the principle is the same for those behind the pulpit.

It makes no difference that a man carries the title of *Reverend* or *Doctor*. Spiritually, he is no different from a plumber or truck driver. If he is saved, he has two natures: the old nature and the new. Just as a born-again plumber must walk in the spirit to overcome the lust of the flesh, so must the pastor or college president. There is no difference. The simple prescription which God makes available to all, high or low, famous or unknown, is the Word of God. Without a continual, yea daily, consumption of the Word, a college president can be as prone to pornography as a teamster. Without meditating in the Word day and night, a pastor is no less prone to the charms of another woman than a construction worker. Thy word have I hid in mine heart that I might not (yea, will not) sin against thee.

And so, a simple but profound preventative for moral failure is the daily, yea day and night, consumption of the Word of God. This is true for whatever station in life one is. Saturating our minds with the Word will enable us to walk in the spirit, precluding fulfilling the lusts of the flesh. Filling our minds with the Word will influence our hearts so that we *will not* sin against God. It is as simple as that.

Notwithstanding, I can already hear some complain: "That's fine for you Sorenson. But I just don't have time to be in the Word to the degree which you describe." My rejoinder therefore is, then you don't have time to prevent moral failure in your life. Like a terrorist who only has to succeed once in blowing up a building, the devil only has to succeed once in tripping you up with temptation.

Most spiritual leaders who fall morally did not get up one morning and think, "Today, I am going to succumb to temptation." (Now after the initial fall, when repeating the sin may not seem to matter anymore, one might even plan the next foray into his sin. That is not what I am speaking of here.) Most Christian leaders do not initially plan for moral failure. But if one is not walking in the spirit, filling his mind with the Word, temptation can and will sneak up.

* * * * *

A well-known pastor, while driving in a far side of his area, thought no one would ever know if he slipped into the "Gentlemen's Club" (read strip joint) across the way. The entry and parking area were shielded by the building, so as not to be easily seen from the highway. Therefore, no one likely would see him. No one knew him in that part of town anyway.

Waiting at the stoplight, he observed a woman who likely was one of the strippers crossing the parking lot on her way to work. She was attractive and shapely. As he thought about it, he considered it would be a rush to see her performing in the club. The tempter had set his trap. The preacher took the bait. Looking around to see who might be watching, the preacher pulled into the parking lot behind the building. He took off his coat and tie, put on sun glasses, grabbed a baseball cap out of the backseat, and slipped into the strip joint. On his way out, he bought X rated DVDs to play on his laptop.

Though he got away with this first foray into moral failure, eventually he will be caught. Somebody will recognize him. Somebody will find out. Sin has a nasty way of finding itself out, especially sin of this nature.

Meanwhile, a not-well-known pastor from a smaller church in the area was one who saturated his mind and heart with the Word of God on a regular, day-in day-out discipline. Later that week he passed the same intersection and the same scenario and the same temptation presented itself. His immediate reaction was NO and he drove on. He was walking in the spirit.

Though his flesh may have found the prospect of a strip show enticing, he refused to even consider the matter. It was not even debatable. Moreover, he knew in his heart the terrible consequences of succumbing to such sin. His life, ministry, and testimony would be ruined. His marriage would be shaken. His family embarrassed. His income likely would cease. Yielding to such temptation would not only be wrong, it would be heavy-duty stupid. The answer was NO!! There really was no tug. His heart was focused on the things of God rather than on the lust of his flesh. He drove on, not giving the "Gentlemen's Club" a second thought.

What was the difference in these two scenarios? In the first, the well-known preacher, though giving lip service to the Word of God really did not absorb significant quantities thereof personally. He used the Bible as a reference book to prepare sermons and lessons. He had nominal devotions on an irregular basis. Besides, he was so busy with all the various ministries which he oversaw, he did not have time (he thought) to absorb large portions of the Word. He had deceived himself into thinking that because he was a well-known spiritual leader, he would never delve into such sin. The devil knew better.

In the second scenario, the not-well-known preacher routinely, yea day and night, filled his mind with the Word of God. It kept him walking in the spirit. It kept his mind set on things above. It influenced his heart so that he would not even contemplate yielding to such temptation. Eventually, the preacher in the first scenario was found out and was ignominiously put out of the ministry. The second preacher, though largely obscure, insofar as having a national reputation was concerned, continued on serving God the rest of his life.

Chapter Notes

[1]That seminar was the Institute for Basic Youth Conflicts. I do not endorse the ministry of Bill Gothard today. Our visit to his seminar in 1972 was the one and only time we attended.

[2]Psalm 1:3

[3]Psalm 119:97

[4]Colossians 3:16

[5]Joshua 1:8

[6]Daniel 1:8

[7]Psalm 1:3

[8]That conference was held at Faith Baptist Church in LaCrosse, Wisconsin. I belief Dr. Max Weniger was the pastor at that time.

[9]I Corinthians 2:16

[10] I used the generic term *newsletter* here rather than the proper title of the e-publication.

Chapter 5
The Prevention of Prayer

Walking in the Spirit such that we walk not in the flesh in reality is basic Christianity. The principles involved are not advanced or complex. It goes back to the basics we learned (or should have learned) not long after we were saved. We teach young converts how they need to spend time in the Word *and* in prayer. God speaks to us through His Word while we speak to Him in prayer. This is Christianity 101. Nevertheless, these principles are intrinsic to walking in the spirit and getting victory over sin.

Luke 22:40,46

In Gethsemane, Jesus directed His disciples, "*Pray that ye enter not into temptation.*"[1] Jesus then knelt and poured out His heart to His heavenly Father in pathos-laden prayer. The focal point of the ages was at hand. He was about to be delivered to His foes for crucifixion and He knew it. He was about to become sin who knew no sin. Sin was about to be judged in His body. Hence, He resorted in prayer to His only refuge and strength – His Heavenly Father. However, prior thereto, He directed His very-human disciples to pray.

The inspired grammar is instructive. The verb translated as "pray" is προσευχομαι (*proseuchomai*). It means "to pray." Further, it is conjugated as an imperative, in the middle voice. Jesus ordered His disciples to pray in that fateful hour. For His part, He was about to go to prayer. He therefore gave an order to His disciples: "You fellows *yourselves* go to prayer so that ye enter not into temptation." More grammar. The verb "enter" is translated from the word εισερχομαι (*eiserchomai* – to enter) and is in the infinitive mode.

(Please bear with me in all this technical grammatical stuff. It is insightful in rightly understanding what Jesus said.) The thought is not, "pray and ask God to not be tempted." A surface reading might suggest that but it is not what Jesus meant. Rather, our Lord in essence said to His disciples, "Meanwhile, you fellows go to prayer *so that* you enter not into temptation." The thought is that time spent in prayer in and of itself would preclude temptation. Though their temptation that night certainly would not be sexual in nature, temptation was just ahead. The temptation to forsake Jesus and flee was just around the corner. In fact, all but Peter and John did just that. And, when confronted over being a disciple, Peter then yielded to the temptation to deny his Lord, even with profanity. In the heated confrontation just ahead in the garden, Peter succumbed to the temptation to retaliate by trying to cut off someone's head with his sword. He missed and only took off the ear of the high priest's servant when the poor fellow ducked.

Ironically, the disciples rather went to sleep. The hour was late. It no doubt had been a long day. Their spirit was willing, but their flesh was weak. As Jesus knelt nearby, agonizing in prayer, sweating as it was great drops of blood, His disciples were curled up a short distance away asleep.

Not long thereafter, Jesus returned to them and asked, *"Why sleep ye? rise and pray, lest ye enter into temptation."*[2]

However, as He spake, Judas and the authorities arrived. Peter could not resist the temptation to retaliate. It was a reaction rooted in the flesh. However, if he had been praying rather than sleeping, he likely would have been in the spirit and not in the flesh. In so doing, he would not have succumbed to the carnal temptation to retaliate.

We likely will not be in that precise temptation. However, we all will and do face temptation of other varieties, notably sexual temptations. Yet, the greater principle enunciated by our Lord in the garden continues to this day. Prayer is a simple means to preclude temptation of whatever variety, certainly sexual. When we are in prayer, we will rise above the realm of the flesh to that of the spirit. We may not always be able to be in the Word, or even meditate therein, but we can always pray regardless of the situation. In rising to the realm of the spirit, we effectively at that moment are walking in the spirit. Recall the promise of Galatians 5:16, "*This I say then, Walk in the Spirit, and ye shall not fulfil the lust of the flesh.*"

Furthermore, when we are in prayer, our thoughts are elsewhere. We are on a different frequency and on a different wavelength. The enticements of the flesh don't operate on that frequency. My wife and I are boaters. We spend as much time in the summer as we can on our boat. At the helm station, we have two fixed-mount VHF marine-band radios for general communications and for emergency use. There are a number of government-assigned marine radio frequencies. If our radio is set to channel 68, for example, I will not hear a call on channel 16, the standard call channel. The radio is not listening on that frequency.

And so it is spiritually. When we are in prayer, we will not hear the devil's siren song of temptation. It's on a different frequency – a different channel. Prayer will lift us up out of the realm of the flesh and into that of the spirit. When we are on that "channel," we will not get the various signals of temptation. They are on the channel of the flesh.

Let us consider a different analogy. When we are on the line, in prayer, talking to our heavenly Father, the devil can't get through. The line is busy. It is as simple as that. "*Pray that ye enter not into temptation.*" This is Christianity 101.

Let us therefore consider several other passages of Scripture regarding prayer. They are insightful.

I Thessalonians 5:17

The Apostle Paul wrote to the church at Thessalonica, "*Pray without ceasing.*" This, though one of the shortest verses in the Bible, contains a powerful principle indeed. Once again, this verse is an imperative. That is, it is a command of God. We are commanded to pray continuously. The word translated as "without ceasing" is αδιαλειπτωος (*adialeiptos).* It means, "without intermission, incessantly, or without ceasing." The simple truth is that God would have us in prayer continuously.

The thought is not that we are to be on our knees all our waking hours. Rather, as we go about our daily tasks, we are enjoined to routinely and frequently touch base with headquarters. There are numerous things for which we should routinely pray: praise, thanks, guidance, direction, and confession. Then, there is the endless list of people we know, all of whom have various needs: spiritual, physical, emotional. Some are lost and need to be saved. Some are babes in Christ and need to grow. Some are struggling spiritually. Some have serious health issues. The list in endless. We can and ought to pray as we go about our daily tasks.

Frequently, as I drive around town on routine errands, I turn the radio off and pray as I drive. There always is a need for guidance and wisdom. There is always a need to praise and thank God for his goodness. There frequently is a need to confess an angry or bitter thought, not to mention a cross word which passed over my lips. As I drive to visit someone, particularly if there is the potential for spiritual conflict, I pray for the help of the Holy Spirit. There may be need for conviction by the Spirit of an unsaved party. There may be need of wisdom on my part and conviction of the Spirit on the part of a backslidden Christian. There frequently is a need to pray and ask God to open doors or to bind Satan so as not to interrupt an attempt to present the Gospel.

As I go on a daily aerobic walk each afternoon, I frequently pray. There are a number of basic desires of my heart which I rehearse before the Lord each day. If at no other time, I can do that while walking. At times, I may awaken during the night and not immediately go back to sleep thereafter. It is an ideal time to pray though my head is on the pillow. (Interestingly, praying during the night is a good sedative. I usually fall back asleep in prayer.) As I sit waiting for my turn in the barber chair, I can close my eyes and pray. The same is true while waiting for the doctor or dentist.

We can pray in most situations. We are enjoined to do so in I Thessalonians 5:17. Such is a simple, yet effective, means of walking or living in the spirit. As we walk in the spirit, we will not fulfill the lusts of the flesh.

Colossians 4:2

Nearing the conclusion of his epistle to the Ephesians, the Apostle wrote, *"Continue in prayer, and watch in the same with thanksgiving."* The thought is again an imperative. It is a court order inspired by the Holy Spirit. The tense is present, indicating continuous action. We are thus commanded by God to be continually in prayer, being careful to offer thanksgiving to God. The thought closely parallels that of I Thessalonians 5:17. Continual, ongoing prayer is a basic commandment for the Christian life. It also is an effective prevention against temptation of whatever variety, certainly moral failure.

Ephesians 6:18

As the Apostle Paul concluded his great description of Christian armor in Ephesians 6, he added, "*Praying always with all prayer and supplication in the Spirit, and watching thereunto with all perseverance and supplication for all saints*." The initial thought literally is "praying at all times." Moreover, that praying is to be in the Spirit. Furthermore, they were directed to persevere therein. That is, keep on praying for God's people and for the Apostle himself (verse 19). Many more comments could be made at this juncture. However, what is particularly significant is that the inspired injunction to be "praying always" is in the context of spiritual armor. It is protective. It will help deflect and quench the fiery darts of the wicked one. It will be part of the armor of righteousness in preventing moral failure.

The principles are simple. It is not rocket science. Walk in the spirit and we will not fulfill the lust of the flesh. That is accomplished in part by filling our minds with the Word of God to the degree it soaks down into our heart. It also is accomplished by having a continual attitude of prayer – praying always.

* * * * *

Paul's Prayer Life

Paul practiced what he preached. In his various epistles, he indicated that he prayed continuously. In I Corinthians 1:4, he wrote, "*I thank my God always on your behalf.*" He wrote to the Philippian church, "*I thank my God upon every remembrance of you, Always in every prayer of mine for you all making request with joy*" (Philippians 1:4).

The Apostle wrote to the Colossian church, "*We give thanks to God and the Father of our Lord Jesus Christ, praying always for you*" and then "*we also, since the day we heard it, do not cease to pray for you*" (Colossians 1:3, 9).

He wrote the Thesssalonian church, "*We give thanks to God always for you all*" (I Thessalonians 1:2). He also wrote to them "*Wherefore also we pray always for you*" (II Thessalonians 1:11). In I Thessalonians 3:10, the Apostle wrote, "*Night and day praying exceedingly.*" Finally, Paul wrote Timothy that, "*without ceasing I have remembrance of thee in my prayers night and day*" in II Timothy 1:3.

Paul prayed day and night. It should be no surprise that there is no record of moral failure or any other character flaw on his part.

The Apostle Paul, arguably, was the greatest Christian who ever lived. He was a man who was continuously in prayer. A similar pattern is found in the Psalms as David described how he cried out to God day and night. Sadly, there came a time in David's life when he failed morally. Though we are not informed of his daily practices at that time, it is safe to conclude, it was a time of spiritual backsliding when he was not in the Word or prayer as he ought.

* * * * *

The Prevention of Prayer

Once again, we revisit the idea of daily devotions wherein one spends a few minutes in prayer in the morning and reads a few verses of Scripture. I believe that philosophy has done as much damage as good. Little is better than none. Yet, for many a Christian, little time is spent in the Word or prayer. We live in an age of bite-sized Christianity: Christianettes listening to sermonettes, having devotionettes.

The greater scope of Scripture speaks of meditating in the Word day and night and praying without ceasing. As our minds are filled with the Word of God on a daily, yea day-and-night basis, we *will not* sin against God. As we are continually in an attitude of prayer as we go about our daily lives, we will rise to the realm of the spirit where the lusts of the flesh are tuned out. This is basic Christianity. It is the God-ordained pattern for Christian living.

Prayer takes us into the presence of God. There, the devil has no access. There, the cell phone of temptation does not ring. There, we rise above the realm of the flesh. The beautiful thing is that we can pray silently wherever we are and whatever we are doing.

A wonderful illustration of this is found in Nehemiah. Nehemiah was the cupbearer to Artaxerxes, king over the Persian Empire. One day, Artaxerxes asked Nehemiah why his countenance was sad. Nehemiah explained the distress the pilgrim Jews back in Jerusalem faced in the desolate city. To that the king asked, "*For what dost thou make request?*"[3] In effect, the most powerful man on the face of the earth of that day offered Nehemiah a blank check. He in effect asked, well what do you want, implying that he would grant it. At that juncture and moment, we then read, "*So I prayed to the God of heaven.*" As Nehemiah paused to collect his thoughts before Artaxerxes, he fired off a silent prayer to heaven. He may have asked, "O God what shall I ask?" Or, perhaps, he asked, "O God, please give me wisdom." We don't know. But what we do know is that when a momentous opportunity presented itself, Nehemiah paused to slip a silent request to heaven for help.

Here was a man who was accustomed to praying continuously. He had a prayer attitude. It was a small step for Nehemiah to come before the throne of grace to obtain mercy and find grace to help in time of need. His cell phone of prayer was continuously on and heaven's number was always on the screen. All he had to do was press the send key and he was in touch with God. So should our prayer lives be.

As we pray, we will not enter into temptation. We will rise into the realm of the spirit and come into the presence of God. Prayer will keep us walking in the spirit.

* * * * *

When we lived in Florida, it was warm enough most of the year for people to wear swimming suits in public and not a few did. It was not uncommon to see a neighbor woman sunning herself in the tiniest of a bikini across the street or in an adjacent yard. We did not have to go the beach to see such. In driving between our house and the church, it was common to see women out doing yard work in tiny bikinis. Teenage girls would ride their bikes down the street in shorts and a bikini top. My point is that, one did not have to buy pornography. There was soft porn all around. It was easy to see. Even in the suburban community in which we lived, it was not unusual to see a provocatively dressed prostitute on a street corner seeking business. It was a battle to keep my eyes and mind where they ought to be and not allow the lust of the flesh to direct my thoughts. However, I noticed that when I was in prayer as I drove around town, though I might perceive some sexy female in shorts and a bikini top, my thoughts were elsewhere. I was in contact with heaven. I was in the realm of the spirit. The devil could not get through. The line was busy. I was talking to my heavenly father. I was on a different frequency.

We live in a totally different climate in northern Minnesota. However, on warm summer days, some of the same stuff goes on. It is not unusual to see to girls or women without much clothing on a hot day in the summer, especially at a park. When weather is cooler, which it is here most of the time, nevertheless, it is not unusual to see females in tight or otherwise revealing clothing. It is true everywhere. The point is that when a spiritual leader (or a Christian in general) keeps his mind focused in conversation with heaven when out and about, he will not pay any attention to such carnal enticements.

As we pray, we will not enter into temptation. As we pray, we come into the presence of God. As we pray, we will rise into the realm of the spirit. As we live (i.e., walk) in the spirit, we will not fulfill the lust of the flesh. Hence, in praying all the time, there is great prevention against moral failure.

Simple, isn't it!

Chapter Notes

[1]Luke 22:40

[2]Luke 22:46

[3]Nehemiah 2:4

Chapter 6
The Principle of Righteousness

*"By the armour of righteousness
on the right hand and on the left"*

As I began to read the Bible through over and over years ago, several themes began to come to the surface of my mind. Of course, I understood the classic doctrines of basic theology, creation, sin, salvation, as well as how God called a people in Abraham (Israel of the Old Testament) and how He called a people in Christ (the church of the New Testament). But one concept started to come into focus which I had not heard much about in my formal education.[1] That concept was practical righteousness.

In college and seminary, I had learned the lofty truths of imputed righteousness, but no one ever talked much about the simple principle of just doing what was right.[2] Hence, I was surprised to notice how frequently the terms *righteous, upright, just,* and *righteousness* were found in the Bible, not too mention derivative concepts such as justification.

In II Corinthians 6:7, the Apostle Paul was impressed to write, *"by the armour of righteousness on the right hand and on the left."* In the context, the Apostle was describing how among numerous other characteristics, his ministry was verified by the armor of righteousness. Though lifting that phrase out of its context, the simple truth is that there is profound protection in the practice of righteousness. The prophet Isaiah spoke of righteousness as a breastplate.[3] And, of course, the Bible refers to the breastplate of righteousness in Ephesians 6:14. The greater principle is that righteousness, like a shield or breastplate, is spiritual armor. It protects. The arrows of temptation, shot by the devil, will bounce off the armor of righteousness. Accordingly, the principle and practice of righteousness can be profound protection against moral failure.

The Frequency of Righteousness

More than thirty years ago when I began to notice the constant reference to righteousness in the Bible, I sat down one day with an old *Young's Analytical Concordance* of the Bible. I began to count all the times the root concept of righteousness appeared. When considering the several basic root words and variations, I found that the concept of righteousness appears in the Bible more than 1,200 times. On average, that is about once for every chapter in the Bible. By contrast the several words translated as *love* and their derivatives appear less than 475 times. *Grace* appears 159 times. *Mercy* and its derivatives appear 394 times.

The several words translated as *holy* and its derivatives appear about 850 times. The several words translated as *good* and its derivatives appear about 778 times. What is significant is that the concept of righteousness in its various derivative forms appears more than any other descriptive moral concept in the Bible. This therefore is a concept which demands further inquiry, particularly as it becomes a major spiritual defense against sin and moral failure.

In not a few places, members of the Godhead are described as being righteous. For example, Jesus Christ is called righteous in I John 2:1. He is called the Just One in Acts 7:52 as well as Acts 22:14. In Psalm 119:137, the psalmist cried out, "*Righteous art thou, O LORD, and upright are thy judgments.*" Likewise in Psalm 129:4, he cried out, "*The LORD is righteous.*" And again in Psalm 145:17 we read, "*The LORD is righteous in all his ways.*" In John 17:25, Jesus cried out, "*O righteous Father, the world hath not known thee: but I have known thee.*" Likewise, the Holy Spirit is associated with righteousness in a number of places in the Bible such as Romans 8:10.

In various places in the Bible, we read how God loves righteousness or will bless those practicing it. In Psalm 5:12, the psalmist wrote, "*For thou, LORD, wilt bless the righteous; with favour wilt thou compass him as with a shield.*" David wrote, "*For the righteous LORD loveth righteousness; his countenance doth behold the upright*" (Psalm 11:7). In Psalm 33:5, the inspired text says, "*He loveth righteousness and judgment.*" In Hebrews 1:9 we read regarding Christ, "*Thou hast loved righteousness, and hated iniquity.*"

Psalm 45:6 says that the "*the sceptre of thy kingdom is a right sceptre*" and that when Christ returns in power and great glory that "*righteousness shall be the girdle of his loins*" (Isaiah 11:5).

Of further note is the chronicling of the kings of Israel and Judah. In Kings and Chronicles, the Holy Spirit often summarized their reign and their character in terms of righteousness or the lack thereof. For example, in I Kings 15:11, Holy Writ records, "*And Asa did that which was right in the eyes of the* LORD." In II Kings 12:2, the sacred historian wrote, "*And Jehoash did that which was right in the sight of the LORD all his days wherein Jehoiada the priest instructed him.*" Likewise, we read that Hezekiah "*did that which was right in the sight of the LORD, according to all that David his father had done*" (II Chronicles 29:2). Similarly, Josiah "*did that which was right in the sight of the LORD, and walked in the ways of David his father, and declined neither to the right hand, nor to the left.*" In fact, all the great kings of Judah are characterized as having done that which was right in the sight of the Lord.

Conversely, the sacred historian wrote, "*Twenty years old was Ahaz when he began to reign . . . and did not that which was right in the sight of the LORD his God, like David his father.*" In the case of Amaziah, the inspired Writ said, "*he did that which was right in the sight of the LORD, but not with a perfect heart*" (II Chronicles 25:2).

God is righteous. Everything about Him is righteous. He loves it when His people are righteous. The coming reign of Jesus Christ someday is characterized as righteous. Moreover, our salvation is described in terms of righteousness – justification which is imputed righteousness.

However, as mentioned a short while ago, it is my perception that most theological education focuses on the imputed righteousness of our justification and virtually ignores the more basic concept of practical righteousness. Though righteousness in the Book of Romans focuses on imputed righteousness, the vast majority of other references to righteousness in the Bible pertain to practical righteousness. The latter is simply doing what is right. Furthermore, there is an entire theology which pertains to practical righteousness. Part of the value thereof is summarized in II Corinthians 6:7. Righteousness becomes a suit of armor, protecting one from moral failure as well as sin of any other variety.

* * * * *

Nuances of Righteousness

The New Testament principle of righteousness is firmly rooted in the Old Testament. Though there is only one basic Greek New Testament word for *righteous* (δικαιος *dikai-os*), there are at least three words in the Old Testament that describe the greater concept. Each are instructive.

Righteousness of Principle

The most basic word for *righteous* or *righteousness* in the Old Testament is the word צדיק (*tsaddiyq*) or its derivative צדק (*tsedeq).* These terms are used more frequently than any other to describe the principle of righteousness. The thought inherent in both is that of righteousness of principle – doing right simply because it is right. It describes what is right or just in an absolute sense. It is the word used to describe God Himself in Psalm 11:7.[4] God is righteous and all that He does is righteous. Yet, the same term is used to describe God's people who live righteously.

"For thou, LORD, wilt bless the righteous; with favour wilt thou compass him as with a shield" (Psalm 5:12). Imputed righteousness is not in view here. Rather, God particularly loves those who are righteous in their living – in their deeds, thoughts, and words. The individual described here is one whose life is directed by the principle of righteousness and finds its outworking in his conduct. Thus, righteousness as a principle is an absolute virtue. It describes God' nature. It also describes the principle whereby God would have us live our lives.

Righteousness of Practice

A second Hebrew word used frequently in the Old Testament is ישר (*yashar*). It is most frequently translated as "upright" or "uprightness." Whereas צדק (*tsedeq*) refers to righteousness of *principle*, ישר (*yashar*) refers to righteousness of *practice*. The latter develops from the former. The thought is of right living – one whose life is characterized by doing what is right. It refers to righteousness of character – one in which the principle of righteousness has become the practice whereby he lives.

Thus, in Psalm 11:7 again, we read, "*For the righteous LORD loveth righteousness; his countenance doth behold the upright.*" Notice how the principle of righteousness has developed in the practice thereof. The one so described is called upright (ישר *yashar*) at the end of the verse. In such an one, the principle of righteousness has soaked down into his heart to such a degree that his character is now ordered by righteousness. He is called upright.[5]

A similar though different word is sometimes used which is תם (*tom*). Though sometimes translated as upright, it is more frequently rendered as "integrity." Again, the greater thought is of one whose life is ordered by the principle of righteousness such that his character is not only upright, he is described as having "integrity." All of these describe one whose life is ordered by the principle of righteousness.

Several classic examples of upright men in the Bible come to mind. Recall how Daniel "*purposed in his heart that he would not defile himself with the portion of the king's meat, nor with the wine which he drank.*"[6] Here was a young man who refused to compromise the convictions he had been taught by his godly parents. His character was upright because the principle of righteousness had soaked down into his life. Therefore, his integrity and uprightness of heart caused him to courteously and respectfully decline partaking of the king's meat (i.e., likely pork) and the king's wine (i.e., alcoholic beverages). Daniel is a classic example how the principle of righteousness so ordered his life that it produced integrity of character and uprightness of life. He refused to acquiesce to the Babylonian standards. Moreover, he did so courteously and respectfully, suggesting an alternative course of action which was righteous for a Jewish man.

Even more germane to the greater thrust of this book is the story of Joseph and Mrs. Potiphar found in Genesis 39. There, Joseph was offered a golden opportunity to enter a bed of adultery by a willing and seductive woman in Mrs. Potiphar. Though the text does not go into such detail, one can only imagine the immodesty of dress and provocative wiles she used in attempting to seduce Joseph. To the contrary, Joseph cried out, "*How then can I do this great wickedness, and sin against God?*"[7]

Moreover, the inspired text reveals that Joseph "refused" to cooperate with her.[8] His answer was NO! How different history would have been if Joseph had yielded to the temptation. His name would be synonymous with moral failure rather than the uprightness and integrity it has come to reflect.

Once again, here is an example of a man whose life was characterized by righteousness. And that righteousness had so ordered his character that he was upright in the face of great temptation. That uprightness produced integrity of character. It is my view that Joseph did not sink into moral failure because the principle of righteousness ordered his life.

Righteousness of Judgment

A third major concept of righteousness in the Old Testament is that of righteous judgment. The greater thought is of making right decisions. The third major Hebrew word related to righteousness is משפט (*mishpat).* It is usually translated as "judgment," though on eighteen occasions is rendered as "right" and several times as "justice." Again, the basic thought is of making right decisions or of good judgment. Interestingly, it is often paired with the words *justice* or *righteousness.*

In the greater vein of righteousness, the idea of right decisions or good judgment should be obvious when confronted with temptation, especially of an immoral nature. Making the right decision will prevent one from moral failure.

I am mindful of a situation which took place years ago. We had on our staff an individual who was a good man. I certainly do not know all that was in his heart, but the best I could tell, he was a decent man. Alas, he used bad judgment when an attractive female came on the scene. Ted[9] taught in our Christian High School and was well liked by the students. He tried to help them when they struggled academically.

Amanda[10] was a student from a home whose parents desired her to be in a Christian school, but did not have particularly strong convictions regarding modest dress. This seventeen-year-old girl was well developed as a young woman. Furthermore, she had a tendency to wear her clothing tight. Her figure was quite attractive and because of the snugness of her clothing, there was no question about it to any observer. Though the school warned her about the way she dressed, she flaunted her figure on the weekends when not under school discipline.

In the course of events, Ted began to help her for one of her classes in his office on Sunday afternoons, before the evening service. In fact, the tutoring led to a friendship between them which was not wise. Sadly, Ted could not resist the urge to keep his hands off his attractive student and she did not seem to care. Though he thought there was privacy in his office, he forgot there was a small window in his office door. From there, he was observed with his hands on the girl in an inappropriate fashion. This led to Ted's dismissal and as far as I know, he has never again been in a paid position in any ministry.

There was no evidence of full sexual contact. But Ted certainly had exercised wrong judgment. What he did was not right. He should never have been alone in his office with the girl with the door closed in the first place. That was bad judgment. He should never allowed his hands on the girl in any fashion, especially in private, regardless if she did not care. That was bad judgment. Was the girl wrong in wearing tight clothing? Yes. But unto whom much is given, much is required. Ted exercised wrong judgment throughout the whole incident. It cost him his job and his reputation, at least in that community. Right judgment is protection which will serve as a defense from the attack of the devil. It is a form of righteousness.

Uprightness of Character

Uprightness of character will preclude moral failure. And such uprightness, in considerable measure, stems from the Word of God. The source and final authority of righteousness is in the Bible.

As a young man years ago, I heard an old evangelist by the name of Glen Schunk urge young men to read a chapter a day in the book of Proverbs. Because there are 31 chapters in Proverbs, one can readily read the book through in a month. Just before I started the regimen of reading through the Word seven times a year, I read through Proverbs once a month for about a year and a half. I was struck by how frequently the principle of righteousness, as well as the more practical matter of uprightness, appeared in Proverbs. Then, I noticed a similar frequency in the Book of Psalms. In fact, about one third of the references to righteousness found in the entire Bible are in Psalms and Proverbs. (Of further interest is that in Proverbs, wisdom and righteousness are essentially equated.[11])

As I then commenced my more extensive Bible reading shortly thereafter, I noticed the principle and practice of righteousness were woven throughout the entire Bible. I came to understand that God wills for His people to always do what is right.[12] As I pondered this concept, it seemed apparent that its profundity was exceeded only by its simplicity. There is nothing complicated about doing what is right. Even a child can understand that. Doing what is right is not rocket science. It does not take a Boston lawyer to determine what is right in most situations.

Accordingly, when our children were young, we taught them over and over, "We always do what's right." If we said that once, we said it hundreds of time over the years. Did they always do what was right? No, nor did we their parents. However, that principle became ingrained in their minds and ours. The principle of righteousness began to be the operative philosophy of our lives.[13] Little by little, doing what was right began to order our lives. It became the "operating system" or operating platform from which the programs of our lives ran. Did we ever do wrong? Yes. Were we sinless? No. But righteousness as a philosophy began to order our lives. When temptation would present itself, I often would ask myself, "Is it right?" If not, the answer was NO. There was nothing complicated about it. There is no doubt in my mind that the philosophy of doing what was right, which came to order my life, prevented this preacher from moral failure on more than one occasion.

Righteousness can also be translated into the simple philosophy of doing as I ought to do. If something is right, then I ought to do it. If I ought to do it, then I should do it. And if I should do it, therefore, I will compel myself to do it. Hence, righteousness is not only a philosophy which will keep me from doing wrong, it becomes a philosophy which develops self discipline – the discipline of doing what I should do, how I should do it, and when I should do it. The principle and philosophy of righteousness therefore will not only keep me from falling, it will constrain me to do as I ought. It will develop discipline of life which becomes a fountain of diverse blessings.

Hence, Christian character is the self discipline to do what is right. It becomes an upward spiral rather than the ugly circle and cycle of sin. As we determine to do what is right, that in itself becomes the armor of righteousness on the right hand and the left. But as our lives become ordered by righteousness, we begin to develop the self discipline to do as we ought. And, that self discipline leads to greater resolve to do what is right. The righteous cycle feeds itself. It is a profound philosophy.

The Ability to Say "NO"

Temptation of an immoral nature will come. The devil will see to that, particularly for those in spiritual leadership. The ability and strength to say NO is crucial. Let us look at another scriptural principle which provides this ability.

In Romans 6:11, the Apostle Paul wrote to the church at Rome and admonished them, *"Likewise reckon ye also yourselves to be dead indeed unto sin, but alive unto God through Jesus Christ our Lord.*" The key concept here is found in the word translated as "reckon." It is translated from the Greek word λογιζομαι (*logidzomai*). It essentially refers to thinking or determining. (As may be apparent, it derives from the familiar term λογος {*logos}*). In this context, it essentially means, "make up your mind." By extension, the thought is to plan in advance or to think it over ahead of time.

Years ago, a good man in our church was an over-the-road truck driver. We live in the north country where forests are the rule. In those forests are plenty of wild life, not the least of which are deer, along with moose, bears, and wolves. Traveling across open stretches of northern Minnesota, Wisconsin, or Upper Michigan, it is not unusual for deer or a bear to run across the highway. There have been countless collisions between vehicles and such creatures over the years. Some drivers attempt to swerve around an animal and wind up in the ditch at the least, crossing the center line into on-coming traffic, or hitting a tree.

Therefore, my truck-driver friend shared his strategy. He told me that he had made up his mind in advance what he would do when an animal ran out in front of his truck. The decision was already made. He would not swerve. If it meant hitting the deer, then so be it. Far better to have a broken headlight or dented fender than swerving and hitting a tree or crossing into on-coming traffic. I don't know if he ever hit any animals, but that simple strategy has stuck with me over the years.

That story illustrates the concept of Romans 6:11. We need to make up our minds in advance that when temptation suddenly crosses our path that the decision is already made. The answer is NO. I don't have to think about it. I don't have to consider the pros and cons as the devil would have me do. I don't need to try and think up an excuse to justify it. The answer is NO. Therefore, as temptation pops up suddenly, the decision is already made.

When a pop-up ad for questionable things suddenly appears on the computer screen, the answer is NO! When an innocent email is opened and there is a pornographic picture advertising a pornographic site, the answer is NO! When driving by a strip joint and noticing an attractive stripper walking in on her way to work, the answer is NO! When curious to check out websites for phone sex or cyber sex, the answer is NO! When a woman through body language or other subtle ways let's it be known that she is available and willing, the answer is NO! When stopped at a stoplight and a prostitute in provocative attire invites me over, the answer is NO! When alone with a member of the opposite sex and the urge arises to make an advance, the answer is NO! When meeting or dealing with a member of the opposite gender and the urge to flirt arises, the answer is NO!

In each case, the decision has already been made. When we reckon ourselves to be dead indeed to sin *in advance*, the answer is already present. Long ago, I made up my mind that when temptation, not only of a sexual nature but also of dishonesty or other forms of wrong, presented itself the answer was already made. It was NO.

Righteousness and Walking in the Spirit

The new nature created within us when we were born again is intrinsically righteous. The sacred text enjoins, "*And that ye put on the new man, which after God is created in righteousness.*"[14] Our new man is righteous. It is inclined to do what is right. It is attuned to the discipline of doing what is right. Righteousness is the operating system by which our new nature functions. There is therefore a symbiotic relationship between the new nature and righteousness. As we develop the principle, practice, and discipline of righteousness to such a degree that it becomes part of our character, we are living parallel to the new nature. Meanwhile, in walking in the spirit, we will be inclined to do right as a matter of principle. One feeds the other. The new nature is righteous in its character and ordering our lives in righteousness keeps us walking in the spirit.

Hence, as we walk in the spirit, we will do what is right. As we order our lives by the principle of righteousness, it keeps us walking in the spirit. Once again, recall the injunction of Galatians 5:16, *"This I say then, Walk in the Spirit, and ye shall not fulfil the lust of the flesh.*" Fulfilling the lust of the flesh is where all moral failure begins. Walking in the spirit is the universal antidote thereto. And, ordering our lives in righteousness reenforces the impetus to walk in the spirit.

I recently took a missions' trip to the Philippines. Our gracious Filipino-pastor host made reservations for us at the best accommodations available in his community. The hotel was directly across the street from where the old Clark Air Force base once was. One afternoon, when I had a little free time, I decided to walk down the street and see the local market place. Little did I know that there were establishments of ill-repute just up the street. They were hangovers from the era of American servicemen. (Our host later warned me that they called that area Sodom and another place near another abandoned US base as Gomorra.)

As I walked up the busy sidewalk of the market place I was accosted by two cute Filipina young women who obviously were either strippers or prostitutes, maybe both. Their apparel (or the lack thereof) made that apparent. They saw a blonde-haired, blued-eyed American (with dollars in my pocket) and immediately solicited me to come into their establishment. It would have been easy to slip into that joint and succumb to lusts of the flesh therein. I was in a foreign country. Nobody knew me. Nobody would know – except One. But the combination of a life long ordered by the discipline of righteousness coupled with walking in the spirit that day made the decision very easy. The answer was NO. It was not even considered. In fact, it was repulsive. I turned around and went back to my hotel.

The Agency of the Word

The principle of righteousness as well as walking in the spirit comes back to the principle of the Word of God. It is the absorption of the Word that gives the strength and impetus to walk in the spirit. Praying transfers me into the realm of the spirit. It is the absorption of the Word of God which produces the impetus and motivation to do what is right. It is the Word of God which continually reminds one of what is right and the reason to do right. And so, these four spiritual virtues all work together for good to provide the impetus to overcome the temptation for moral failure. Yet, the spiritual strength and impetus to walk in the spirit comes from the Word of God and prayer. Likewise, the impetus and spiritual determination to order our lives by the principle of righteousness also comes from the Word of God.

We are back to Christian Life 101. Spending time in the Word and prayer is the secret. As we saturate our minds with the Word to the degree that it soaks down into our hearts, we will not sin against our God. We will walk in the spirit. And, we will order our lives by the principle of righteousness. Moreover, the multitude of other fringe benefits from daily absorption of the Word are numerous. What a wonderful gift our Lord has given us in His Word. *"Man shall not live by bread alone, but by every word that proceedeth out of the mouth of God."*[15]

Chapter Notes

[1]In those years, I had a Bachelor of Arts degree and a Master of Divinity degree.

[2]The reason for that likely was that my instructors were seeking to impress upon their students the great truth of justification by faith and faith alone. Not wanting to cloud that issue, the matter of *doing* what was right was either ignored or assumed to be so basic as to not need further instruction.

[3]Isaiah 59:17

[4]"For the righteous LORD loveth righteousness."

[5]That is not to assume sinless perfection or absolute righteousness. Apart from Jesus, no one has ever achieved this degree. Rather, the thought is the tendency and principle by which one lives can best be described as upright – one who does what is right by principle and habit.

[6]Daniel 1:8

[7]Genesis 39:9

[8]Genesis 39:8

[9]Not his real name.

[10]Not her real name.

[11]See Proverbs 8:1,8, and 20.

[12]Psalm 106:3 " Blessed *are* they that keep judgment, *and* he that doeth righteousness at all times."

[13]Unfortunately, it was to the irritation of some around us who misconstrued our desire to do what was right as self-righteousness.

[14]Ephesians 4:24

[15]Matthew 4:4

Section III – Practical Considerations

Chapter 7
The Protection of Marriage

Thus far, we have examined *spiritual* principles whereby moral failure can be prevented. These have included walking in the spirit, the power of the Word, the prevention of prayer, and the principle of righteousness. Let us in this chapter touch upon a more prosaic principle: the protection of marriage. Without a question, marriage is a gift from God. It is a beautiful union of a man and a woman, bonded together by love and trust. Human marriage certainly is a foreview of the great spiritual marriage between Christ and the church.[1] A godly marriage can and ought to be a self-fulfilling union which is so deep that infidelity is precluded by the intensity of the relationship. It is not the purpose of this chapter to plumb the depths of the implications of a wonderful marriage.[2] However, what is germane to this book is the proposition that a strong marriage relationship of itself can be an added preventative for moral failure in spiritual leadership.

* * * * *

God's Provision

"Now concerning the things whereof ye wrote unto me: It is good for a man not to touch a woman. Nevertheless, to avoid fornication, let every man have his own wife, and let every woman have her own husband."[3] The implication preceding I Corinthians 7 is that the young church at Corinth had written to Paul and inquired as to the propriety of marriage, particularly in regard to sexual relations in the marriage relationship.

Corinth was a city given to open and brazen fornication. On the one hand, it was a busy seaport with transient sailors seeking female consorts while ashore. It also was the seat of a pagan temple which actually utilized female prostitutes as part of the temple "worship." The depraved idea was that Aphrodite, the Greek goddess of love and fertility, would be aroused to send fertility to her adherents in observing her worshipers engaged in sexual intercourse. Hence, the temple of Aphrodite was a huge brothel in Corinth, employing up to 1,000 prostitutes all in the name of "religion." The licentiousness of Corinth was so notorious across the Roman world of the first century that fornication was called "Corinthianizing."

The early Christians at Corinth, in coming to Christ, were convicted of the lasciviousness of their past and were repulsed by it. Some therefore came to the conclusion that sexual relations were immoral altogether, even in the marriage relationship. It was in that environment the Holy Spirit moved the Apostle Paul to write what he did in I Corinthians 7. In verses 1and 2, Paul makes two points. (1) It is not proper for a man to have physical contact with women in general. The thought clcarly is contact of a sexual nature. (2) Therefore, to avoid the burning of impure sexual desires, it was good for people to marry.

Sexual activity in marriage is a given. The clear overview of Scripture is that God has ordained one institution for the righteous and moral fulfillment of sexual desires and that is in the marriage relationship. Though marriage certainly is more than a legal and moral outlet for sexual desires, it is clear that marriage is the context for proper sexual contact between a man and a woman.

Therefore, to answer the question sent to him, Paul endorsed marriage and sexual relations in marriage. Moreover, he made it clear that one purpose of the marriage bed was to preclude fornication. The word so translated here (πορνεια *porneia*) refers to the whole ugly spectrum of sexual impurity: ranging from adultery, to pre-marital sex, to incest, to homosexuality, to any other aberrant form of sexual activity. Hence, a solid, happy marriage, including a strong sex life, is a god-given means of avoiding moral failure.

Accordingly, the Apostle wrote in verse 9, *"But if they cannot contain, let them marry: for it is better to marry than to burn."* Again, the thought is that marriage is a righteous forum to preclude the burning of impure sexual lust. It is a provision of God. Marriage is more than just a place for sex, but it certainly is that. When, for whatever reason, that God-given provision is constricted; the potential for yielding to temptation is increased.

There is never any justification for adultery, pornography, or other acts of moral failure. However, when it has happened, in the dark shadows there sometimes is an untold secret. That secret is that intimacy in the marriage bed had cooled or evaporated altogether for the guilty parties. In such cases, when temptation provided itself, the party was more inclined to yield thereto.

It is no surprise then to this author that one of the conditions for a pastor is that he be the husband of one wife.[4] Though this usually is interpreted to mean a man married more than once should not be a pastor, the fact he should be married in the first place should be obvious. An unmarried man certainly can serve God. The Apostle Paul is the classic example. However, an unmarried pastor certainly limits his ability to minister to the opposite gender. And, he certainly may be more prone to the tempter's snare. Some men do walk in the spirit to such a degree that they will never fulfill the lusts of the flesh. However, in most cases, it is God's plan for a man in spiritual leadership to be married.

God's Protection

> "*The wife hath not power of her own body, but the husband: and likewise also the husband hath not power of his own body, but the wife. Defraud ye not one the other, except it be with consent for a time, that ye may give yourselves to fasting and prayer; and come together again, that Satan tempt you not for your incontinency.*"[5]

Basic advice for the marriage relationship is at hand. God has so ordained that a wife should be willing and available to fulfill her husband's desire for intimacy. Likewise, a husband should be willing and available to satisfy his wife's desire for intimacy. It is a basic principle for the marriage relationship. Then, the Apostle adds, "*Defraud ye not one the other.*" The word translated as "defraud" (αποστερεω *apostereo*) essentially has the thought of "deprive." The idea is that a wife or husband ought not deprive the other of desired sexual intimacy. In fact, the idea is stronger than deprivation. To deprive a spouse of desired intimacy is in fact to defraud them of a God-given protection. God has ordained the marriage bed, in part, to deflect the tempter's snare.

Though a couple might mutually agree to temporarily "fast," regarding marital intimacy, the Apostle makes it clear that this should only be a temporary pause. Fasting from solid food is always a temporary situation, so should be abstinence of intimacy in the marriage bed. The inspired text clearly states, that a married couple should therefore "*come together again.*"

Then, the Holy Spirit impressed upon the Apostle to write, "*that Satan tempt you not for your incontinency.*" That is a powerful statement! The word translated as "incontinency" (ακρασια *akrasia*) has the sense of "a lack of self control" or "intemperance." When a married couple accustomed to ongoing sexual intimacy stops, Paul says they become a target for the devil to tempt them.[6] Regular sexual intimacy in a marriage relationship is an added protection from the snare of the tempter. In addition to the spiritual principles enunciated in earlier chapters of this book, regular intimacy in marriage diminishes the effectiveness of the devil's ability to tempt. Therefore, intimacy in the marriage relationship is another layer of God-given protection against moral failure. A cooling or diminishing of romance for a married couple can be a dangerous thing. It can set one up for attack by Satan.

Pastor Ness[7] had been married for twenty years. Yet, his marriage had been tenuous. He had a hot temper and vented it on his wife with some regularity. She in turn retreated into her own private world. They would bicker and fight over issues ranging from finances to his time spent playing golf. Because a richness of sexual fulfillment in the marriage bed is usually predicated upon a unity of spirit and friendship otherwise, the sexual element of their marriage also faded. Moreover, in the early years of their marriage, Mrs. Ness had tried very hard to keep her weight down to be attractive for her husband. But now with their marriage little more than a cold war, she really didn't care anymore. She put on weight and lost much of the attractiveness of youth she once had. There was no longer any spark in their sex life and the regularity thereof was infrequent.

Pastor Ness was not looking for an illicit love affair. Though he certainly manifested other works of the flesh in losing his temper and belittling his wife, he had always been moral sexually. All pastors at one time or another have had a "strange" woman communicate interest in one way or another. Some women are attracted to men in leadership and the devil knows it. But the fact Pastor Ness's own marriage was unhappy and unfulfilled in the bedroom made him a target for the devil.

Pastor Ness would stop at a donut shop for a cup of coffee several times a week. In so doing, he became friends with one particular waitress. She was slim, trim, and had a pretty smile. Moreover, she wore her clothing snug to reveal her attractive figure.

His eyes would follow her around the room as she did her duties. She picked up on that and began to flirt with him. He in turn became infatuated with her. One day, he asked for her phone number and that evening called and asked if they could get together sometime. His rationale ostensibly would be that he wanted to invite her to church. Well, they met and it soon degenerated into an adulterous affair.

There is no justification for adultery. None. However, the sad secret of Pastor Ness's life was the fact that there no longer was any romantic intimacy in his own marriage. It was as much his fault as his wife's. For him, probably more. But the simple fact is, the provision which God has created to fulfill normal sexual desires is in the marriage bed. When that provision is constricted, the evil one has a greater target. Pastor Ness had failed morally and was no longer blameless in the ministry. Once again, the devil sat and laughed.

* * * * *

Phil Wesley[8] had been in the ministry for well over twenty years. He had come to pastor a church of some size on the West Coast. His name was well-known in the circles of which that church was a part. His wife of all those years was an example of propriety and modesty. She was a good woman.

Yet, Mrs. Wesley had somewhere or other picked up on the idea that sexual intimacy in marriage was primarily for procreation and was a necessary evil to be otherwise tolerated or even avoided.[9] She therefore reluctantly "accommodated" her husband. Her attitude was that it was a domestic "duty" to be endured. She had an obligation to be intimate with her husband, but that was as far as it was going to go. Needless to say, the Wesleys did not have a very strong sexual bond. Their intimacy was perfunctory and infrequent. Mrs. Wesley justified her coolness by her determination to be a modest and chaste woman.

Meanwhile, Pastor Wesley hired a new secretary named Shelly[10]. She had graduated some years earlier from a well-known Christian college, renowned for its high moral standards. She made herself attractive and was quite feminine. Her dress was always modest and appropriate.

Shelly was a warm-hearted woman. She sought to be helpful and went out of her way to please the pastor. She was thoughtful and kind. Pastor Wesley tried to maintain proper decorum in his relationship as her boss. Though there never was any inappropriate overture on her part, the warmth and sweetness of this pleasant woman did not escape Pastor Wesley. She went out of her way to be submissive to his authority and was always cheerful.

Yet, Shelly was lonely. She was single and longed for a husband. One day, Pastor Wesley could not resist the urge to compliment her on how attractive she looked. She was pleased by his compliment. Little by little their relationship began to evolve from strictly professional to personal. He began to tell her his problems and she hers. They began to become emotionally attached. Thoughts of endearment began to grow. That eventually led to friendly touches and then to an inevitable embrace behind closed doors. When that happened Shelly melted in his arms. The long-frustrated intimacy in Pastor Wesley's marriage found a warm and willing recipient in his secretary. Their adultery destroyed his marriage, his ministry, and his testimony.

Yet, in this case, a wife who denied her husband regular and warm intimacy in bed had set her husband up for the tempter's snare. Because of the "frigidness" of their marriage bed, Satan was able to successfully tempt Pastor Wesley and destroy his ministry. A warm and regular relationship in the marriage bed is a God-given protection against moral failure.

God's Plan

"*The heart of her husband doth safely trust in her, so that he shall have no need of spoil.*"[11] These are the words of the sacred text, describing the virtuous woman in Proverbs 31. King Lemuel describes in great detail one whom he called a "virtuous woman." Though that description at first glance seems to describe a woman of pure morals, that actually is not the primary thought. The major thought, both of the etymology of the original language as well as the lengthy description, is of an industrious, hardworking woman who helped support the family.

Notwithstanding, the inspired text says, "*The heart of her husband doth safely trust in her.*" The virtuous woman of Proverbs 31 surely was industrious and hardworking. But the sacred writer makes a point to note that her husband had complete trust in her. Implicit is her fidelity and moral purity.

However, the scriptural penman then wrote, "*so that he shall have no need of spoil.*" The word translated as "spoil" (שלל *shalal*) in this context refers to a female slave girl (perhaps a prisoner of war) taken to be a concubine. Yet, the husband of this virtuous woman had no "need" of such spoil. (1) The context is of marriage and (2) particularly of marital fidelity – the husband safely trusting his wife. Therefore, (3) he had no need or interest for a concubine – the spoil or booty of war.

What is clearly implied is that the virtuous woman of Proverbs 31 satisfied the sexual desires of her husband. He had no need or desire for another woman. Earlier in this book, we have touched upon lofty spiritual principles such as the power of the Word of God, the prevention of prayer, the principle of righteousness, and the potential of the new nature. However, here we have landed and are taxiing up to a simple but frank truth. It is the assertion of this writer that God has ordained for a wife – yea a godly wife – to satisfy and fulfill her husband's sexual desires. When she does, there will be little interest in some other source of sexual gratification.

When a woman, yea even a godly wife, does not fulfill that role, a husband is more prone to impure proclivities. That never justifies moral failure – ever. However, the absence of sexual satisfaction in a marriage does make it easier for the tempter to succeed. In the case of the virtuous woman of Proverbs 31, her husband had no need or interest in another woman. Why? His wife met and satisfied his sexual interests.

Consider this analogy. We all have attempted dieting on occasion. I recently determined that I needed to lose some weight. It was January and after the holiday season when I partook of too many goodies. Therefore, I embarked on a simple diet of no sweets or deserts, no bedtime snacks, no between-meal tidbits and temperance in what I ate at meal time. The truth of the matter is that I often went away from the table slightly hungry. By the next meal time, my stomach was quite hungry. I was in a constant state of being hungry. After a couple of weeks of that diet, I had a powerful urge to eat something sweet. It frankly was a struggle. One day, I yielded to temptation and broke my diet. I succumbed to the urge to eat a chocolate desert my daughter had made.

The analogy is not perfect and there certainly are moral implications involved with immoral acts which do not encumber eating a piece of chocolate cake. But the parallel should be apparent. When a married man, accustomed to a degree of sexual satisfaction, is put on a "diet" in that regard, the urge to eventually satisfy that appetite becomes strong. That never justifies moral failure. But the appetite remains.

The Bed Undefiled

In Hebrews 13:4, we read, "*Marriage is honourable in all, and the bed undefiled.*" The context is not only of marriage, but of the marriage bed. The Bible teaches that sexual intimacy between husband and wife in the marriage bed is honorable and undefiled. The Augustinian philosophy that sexual relations between spouses are only for the purpose of procreation is flawed. To be sure, procreation is one purpose of the marriage bed. However, both Scripture as well as common experience suggest that sexual intimacy in marriage is the ultimate union between a man and wife. The Song of Solomon is a clear scriptural example thereof.

Though marriage is a union on a spiritual as well as emotional level, it certainly is also a physical union, yea a sexual union. To suggest that sexual union should only take place to produce children flies in the face of both Scripture and common experience.

Sexual intimacy in marriage is a deep bond between husband and wife. God intended such intimacy. He in fact is the inventor of sex. Of course, the one place God has ordained for such intimacy is between husband and wife. Notwithstanding the fact the world routinely cheapens and sullies the purity of sex with all of its perversions and immoral activities, sexual intimacy in marriage is a God-given gift to be enjoyed regularly by a married couple.

The Bible enjoins numerous restrictions and regulations on sexual activities. The Levitical Law of the Old Testament records specific prohibitions or regulations regarding sexual practices for Israel. However, there is nary a word regulating sexual intimacy between a husband and wife.[12] Hence, a husband or wife should never consider sexual intimacy, apart from procreation, to be something dirty or impure. To do so sets up the prospect for temptation. Augustine was wrong on a lot of things, Catholic theology not the least. He was wrong on this issue also.

A Strong Marriage

Pastor Howard Blomberg[13] married a lovely young woman some decades ago. Their marriage meanwhile has been a taste of heaven on earth over the years. They have served together in the ministry throughout their entire adult lives and their love for each other is deeper today than it has ever been. There has never been moral failure on the part of Pastor Blomberg. And there are several reasons why.

First, he developed and practiced the spiritual principles described earlier in this book. He endlessly filled his mind with the Word of God, day in and day out, over the years. He consciously sought to walk in the Spirit each day. He sought to order his life by the principle of righteousness. He prayed without ceasing. But there is another reason which is more prosaic. His wife made it easy for him to be faithful and pure.

Mrs. Blomberg, even after decades of marriage, kept herself slim and trim. She remained physically attractive. Though she excelled as a chef, mother of their children, and as homemaker; she also was a romantic lover to her husband.

Sexual intimacy between Pastor and Mrs. Blomberg, even after decades of marriage, remained frequent and passionate. Even after many years of marriage, they joked between themselves that they were still on their honeymoon when in the bedroom. Mrs. Blomberg not only made herself available to her husband for intimacy, she did so willingly, yea eagerly. Moreover, she not infrequently was the instigator thereof. Pastor Blomberg's dear wife utterly fulfilled his sexual desires. *He had no need of spoil.*

And that is the way, I believe, it should be. As the inspired text of Proverbs says, *"he shall have no need of spoil."* Pastor Blomberg had long ago made up his mind that the answer was NO when the devil would waft breezes of temptation before him. He had determined to walk in the spirit and not fulfill the immoral lusts of his flesh. He had years ago ordered his life by the principle of righteousness and reduced temptation to the simple equation it was not right, period.

There had been occasions over the years when a woman made it apparent to Pastor Blomberg that she was available and willing if he was interested. His convictions, however, were strong. His attractive, pure wife certainly made it easy for him to achieve his objective of moral purity. She completely satisfied his sexual desires in their marriage bed.

Mrs. Blomberg continued to keep herself trim. Even as a middle-aged woman, she made it a point to buy and wear sexy lingerie for her husband's eyes only. She would go and buy such undergarments and then model them for her husband behind closed bedroom doors. Though in public, Mrs. Blomberg was the epitome of modesty and a paragon of conservative dress, in the privacy of their marriage bedroom she was not. Pastor Blomberg saw his wife in her "sexy" and skimpy lingerie each morning when they were dressing and each evening as they prepared to retire. In fact, Mrs. Blomberg made a point that her husband saw her so attired. In the privacy of their bedroom, she was slim, trim, and sexy. That is frank, but it also is the truth.

When Pastor Blomberg stopped for gas at a convenience store and there was a rack of pornographic magazines beside the counter, his answer was NO. Not only was it wrong, why did he need that kind of garbage? He could righteously gaze upon his own beautiful wife that night at home. When passing a "gentlemen's club" or "adult" bookstore on the highway, there was no tug to stop. Why get involved with that filth? He would see something better that night in his own bedroom.

Pastor Blomberg knew how easy it was to find pornography on the internet. Apart from the wrongness of so doing, why look at those harlots? His pure, faithful wife was better. He knew. He saw her getting dressed and undressed each day. Furthermore, she was always ready for intimacy and he knew it. *He had no need of spoil.*

When Pastor Blomberg would go on a trip out of town, he knew his wonderful wife would be waiting when he got home. When the children were still living at home, upon arriving from a trip, he knew his wife would soon take him to the bedroom. She told the kids, daddy needed to take a nap and mommy wanted to spend a little time with him. She did.

After the kids were grown and gone, when he came home from a trip, she was waiting for him. And Pastor Blomberg knew it. He always wondered how his wife would appear when he walked in the door. He rarely was disappointed. He would call her on his cell phone about an hour before arriving home and let her know his estimated time of arrival. When he got home, he was met by a woman ready for romance. *He had no need of spoil.*

And so, though Pastor Blomberg had high moral standards and spiritual principles which enabled him to stay pure, his wife surely made it easy for him to do so. Sadly, in some situations that is not the case.

In a number of the unfortunate stories found throughout this book, I have been privy to the details. There is never any justification for moral failure. Nevertheless, in some of those stories, I know it was easier for a spiritual leader to morally fail because there was a barrenness in his own marriage bedroom. That does not justify one's sin. But in some cases, if a man's wife had taken care of herself and been the lover to him which God intended, he may not have failed as he did.

God has ordained that marriage, among other things, be a means of protection from moral failure. The precept in this chapter is not as lofty as the spiritual principles discussed earlier, but it is a crucial part of the armor of righteousness on the right hand and on the left.

Chapter Notes

[1]See Ephesians 5:32

[2]See David Sorenson, *Have a Heavenly Marriage*, (Murfreesboro, TN, Sword of the Lord Publishers, 2000)

[3]I Corinthians 7:1-2

[4]I Timothy 3:2

[5]I Corinthians 7:4-5

[6]A case might be made that an unmarried virgin of either gender is less prone to sexual temptation than a person who is married, accustomed to intimacy, and then deprived thereof.

[7]Once again, this is a fictitious name.

[8]Once again, a fictitious name.

[9]This is the philosophy of Augustine and has been taught in Catholic churches for centuries. Unfortunately, some Protestants and even some Baptists have picked up on this unscriptural philosophy.

[10]Again, a fictitious name.

[11]Proverbs 31:11

[12]The one exception is the discouragement of intercourse during the menstrual period. However, that seems to be more regulatory discouragement than outright prohibition.

[13]Again a fictitious name.

Chapter 8
Why Spiritual Leaders Fail Morally

The tragic litany of spiritual leaders who have experienced moral failure is staggering. In every circle, every fellowship, and every association there is someone. The frequency of such faltering is increasing. No group is immune. Famous leaders receive national attention, in some cases by the secular media. Yet, for every well-known leader falling into moral failure, there are a multitude of relatively unknown spiritual leaders doing the same. Has there always been such a rate of immorality of spiritual leaders? I think not. Fifty years ago, news of such disgraces were few and far between. What has happened? Let us look at a number of reasons.

Decline of Morality in General

Western culture has nose dived in its sexual morality in the past forty years. Presumably, such moral declension began during the sexual revolution of the 1960s and '70s. Wicked Supreme Court rulings have legalized pornography and lewdness in all forms opening the flood gates of filthy literature. It stocks the shelves of many convenience stores.

It floods the internet. Moreover, the simplicity of downloading pornography in the relative privacy of an office or home via high speed internet makes it very easy for a man to peruse such filth just about anywhere or anytime. For some, it becomes virtually addictive.

With the liberalization of Supreme Court rulings regarding "free speech," strip joints, euphemistically referred to as "gentlemen's club" disgrace cities all over the land. In the community of approximately 150,000 population in which this writer lives, there are at least four places where a man can slip in and watch live nude dancers.

One such establishment in this city was even referred to editorially in the local newspaper in a positive fashion because of its years of operation without other problems such as prostitution. The newspaper lauded the live jazz performed there as a reason one might visit this establishment. The newspaper almost made it sound like wholesome entertainment when contrasting it with another more controversial joint in the local news. Women working in such places are euphemistically referred to as "sex industry workers," deserving of the same fringe benefits of other forms of employment, seemingly legitimizing such filth.

There have always been immoral men and women. Fifty years ago, however, a loose women was more of an exception than the rule. Today, a woman of purity and of high moral standards is the exception. Fornication is accepted as normal. Recently, when doing door-to-door visitation in an area of our city housing many university students, I was struck that 80% of the mailboxes on residences where I stopped had names indicating unmarried male and females cohabiting together. For example, the names of 'John Jones' and 'Sally Smith' on a mailbox was to me a clear indication they in all likelihood were not married, but were living together. And that was the case of about 80% of the places in that neighborhood. Many universities allow cohabitation between unmarried couples in their dormitories.

I recently read the result of a survey that indicated that 95% of American young adults have engaged in pre-marital sex. Young-adult women think nothing of sleeping with a boyfriend or living together with him. TV programs such as "Sex in the City" promote and glorify worldly young women living a promiscuous life style. Such garbage is endless in this perverse generation.

Such immorality is not restricted to the world. It is in the church. We have had the sad occasion to discipline members who openly and brazenly were committing adultery. They were angry that we dared interfere with their "private lives." As a pastor, I have been shocked at how many people on the perimeter of the church – not members but professing Christians who occasionally darken the door of the church – who are living together in fornication or engage in casual sex.

We have been shocked to learn junior high kids are having sex and think of it as normal. They talk openly of it. The checkout lanes at any supermarket are filled with magazines with soft pornography on the covers and lurid articles on the inside. In walking by a public transit terminal in our city, it is dismaying to hear the filthy language. What is even worse is that much, if not most, of it comes from adolescent girls, who freely lace their conversations with the F word.

Several years ago, I was saddened to see a teenage girl who could not have been more than fourteen years old pushing a baby stroller down the sidewalk on a summer day. What shocked me was the inscription across her T shirt. In large block letters was the F word! This was on the main street of our so-called conservative Midwestern city. She strolled along with her baby and her obscene T-shirt as if this all was perfectly normal.

We live in a wicked generation. In this debased and depraved culture, sexual morals are passé. In such an immoral environment, a woman getting involved with another man is no big deal. Unfortunately, it is a big deal when the man is a spiritual leader. He no longer is blameless. In this wicked generation, it is no big deal when a man views pornography on his computer. It is a big deal, however, when a spiritual leader does so. He is no longer blameless.

Jesus described His day as an adulterous generation.[1] If that were so then, how much more so is it today? The temptations for sexual impurity abound. People in the world engage in all forms of sexual immorality and think it is normal. When this writer was a young man forty years ago, men in the work place would talk about their sexual exploits or lusts. Today, not a few *women* routinely talk the same in the work place. My wife has told me of women in the law firm where she works, who in the lunch room, speak openly in mixed company about how they would like to get in bed with so and so.

We recently went into a fast-food place for lunch and a car load of high school kids arrived. To be honest, those teenage girls on lunch break looked like young harlots. They had every intention of exposing their bosoms with the tight, low-cut tops they wore – and they did. Sadly, statistics show that many upperclass high school girls in fact are sexually active.

We live in an evil and adulterous generation and those in spiritual leadership will interact with such immoral values on a regular basis. For those not prepared for such temptation, moral failure lies ahead. Whether it is easily available pornography or women who have no shame (and their number is legion), the prospect of moral failure is all around. Those in spiritual leadership must be prepared to say NO firmly and repeatedly.

Satanic Attack in Particular

The devil knows that sexual impurity will turn one's heart from God.[2] Therefore, he promotes immoral situations endlessly. However, the devil also knows that he can take a spiritual leader out of the ministry through moral failure. It is the firm conviction of this writer that the devil will therefore set traps of temptation for those in God's work. Those in Christian service may face situations of temptation that others may not.

As noted earlier in this book, this writer has had occasions over the years where I am convinced a shameless woman sought to entice me. The answer was NO. Nevertheless, an attempt was made. I am further of the opinion that those several instances likely were motivated by the devil to knock this preacher out of the ministry. In cases where men have succumbed to moral failure, who knows whether Satanic traps were set. Once again, there is never any justification for moral failure. However, those in spiritual leadership must be aware that the evil one likely will lay traps for them. They have to be ready to say NO.

As this section was being written, I paused momentarily to check my email. There amidst various messages was an advertisement for immoral garbage. It was clever enough that it passed through the online filters. It was immediately deleted. How that spammer got my email address, I don't know. But the devil likely does.

The good news is that the Bible says, "*Resist the devil, and he will flee from you*" (James 4:7). It is the view of this writer that as we consistently resist the devil, he will give up and try someone else. He is not persistent and will go elsewhere when the target of his temptation consistently says NO. Notwithstanding, some men fail morally because of the specific attack of the devil. That does not mitigate their culpability. But it should make us all the more alert to his wiles.

Walking in the Flesh and not the Spirit

As noted earlier in this book, the works of the flesh are manifest which are these: adultery, fornication, uncleanness, lasciviousness.[3] Without exception, any Christian who ventures into immoral activities is living in the flesh – his old nature, period. Its true whether the guilty party is a backslidden, immature, carnal young Christian. It is equally as true if the guilty party is a Bible college or seminary president. The common denominator is that they are walking in the flesh. It is as simple as that! Titles, position, degrees whether earned or honorary, are meaningless in this conflict.

The simple spiritual solution is to walk in the spirit and we *will not* fulfill the lusts of the flesh![4] God's profoundly simple solution is to walk in the spirit. We have developed this principle in considerable detail earlier. However, the issues of life remain fundamentally spiritual. When a born-again believer puts on the new man, which after God has been created in righteousness and true holiness, he *will not* succumb to the lusts of the flesh. If this is not Christianity 101, it certainly is Christianity 201. It is basic. But each of us need to do so daily and then some.

Sadly, spiritual leaders frequently become encumbered with baggage which sets them up for a fall. It seems the higher one goes in organizational structure, the more liable he is to these weaknesses.

(1) One issue is pride of intellect. Because one has the title *Doctor* or *Reverend* before his name does not keep him walking in the spirit. To the contrary, it might lead in the opposite direction. Once a man receives an advanced degree or title, whether earned or honorary, there is a temptation toward intellectual pride. He is a cut higher than lesser mortals – or so some might think, and some have. Pride is a quick elevator ride down from walking in the spirit. Though few would rationalize they no longer need be concerned with spiritual basics such as walking in the spirit and daily crucifixion of the flesh, that is exactly what happens for some. And they set themselves up for failure.

(2) Busyness of schedule is another piece of baggage easy to pick up as one succeeds in the ministry. Few "laymen" perceive how busy a pastor often is. Furthermore, when a successful preacher becomes the head of an institution of learning, his schedule becomes even busier. The sad truth is that many in high positions of such leadership are too busy. They don't make time for substantial absorption of the Word and extended seasons of prayer. They often have little real time with their wives. Perhaps not by design, but by default, they are too busy to maintain the spiritual basics necessary to actually walk in the spirit. There is only one alternative and that is walking in the flesh. In so doing, they become candidates for the attack of the devil.

I can think of at least one fundamental Baptist spiritual leader in a place of national recognition who drove himself to such an endless schedule that one day he failed morally. He was too busy for extensive time in the Word and prayer. The reality is that on the inside, he was not walking in the spirit. The devil set a trap for him and he took the bait.

(3) A third fault, similar to the first, is ego of position. When a man achieves titles such as reverend, pastor, doctor, and in some cases president, pride of position can creep in. The devil deceives one into thinking that he is above the sin which lesser mortals face. Furthermore, some women are attracted to those in places of spiritual leadership. Yet, "*Pride goeth before destruction.*"[5] Positions of spiritual leadership can seem to be unaccountable. Few would ever articulate such foolishness.

However, there is a subtle nuance when one is the leader. He is the basic authority in an organization. Oh, to be sure, there are oversight boards or the authority of the church itself. But on a day-to-day level, the pastor or president is the chief executive. There thus can be pride of position and pride is a function of the flesh. When a man is weak in walking in the spirit, pride can easily pull him back into the old nature. And the works of the flesh are manifest which are these: adultery, fornication, uncleanness, lasciviousness.

I recall a situation years ago when not many people had cell phones. Back in those years, such were the domain of executives and big shots – they were the only ones who could afford them then. One day, I had an appointment for lunch with the pastor of another church. It was not a large church, but this pastor had a large ego. He also had a cell phone. During the course of the lunch, his cell phone rang. He picked it up and stepped away to accept the call. I have every reason to believe that he had his wife (or perhaps his secretary) call at an appointed time during our lunch to give the impression of how important and busy he was. There is little question in my mind of that.

The sad irony is that some years later, this same man was forced to resign his church for "moral improprieties." There is a close correlation between pride and the works of the flesh. The flesh is the flesh. One walking in the flesh will accomplish the works thereof. In his case, it eventually led to those works of the flesh which were of an immoral nature.

God's basic, yet profoundly simple solution is to walk in the Spirit. Below is a summary of the failures of the basic spiritual steps necessary to walk in the spirit. When a spiritual leader accomplishes these simple steps, yea when any believer does, he *will not* fulfill the lusts of the flesh. Sadly, when these simple truths fade into the background, trouble lies ahead.

Casual Absorption of the Word

I am convinced the reason Christians in general and spiritual leaders in particular walk in the flesh and not the new nature is because of casual absorption of the Word. As developed in an earlier chapter, the power of the Word is profound in warding off temptation. As noted earlier, the Bible says, *"Thy word have I hid in mine heart, that I might not sin against thee."*[6]

Every student in a Christian day school has memorized that verse. Sadly, many in spiritual leadership give only lip service thereto. Of all people, those in spiritual leadership need to be in the Word – even more than others. (1) Unto whom much is given, much is required.[7] (2) Those in spiritual leadership have a target on their back. The devil will attack them especially, more so than an average Christian. The evil one is a specialist in laying traps of temptation.

God's simple antidote and armor, in large measure, is the Word. As developed in chapter 4, the intrinsic thought of Psalm 119:11 is so saturating our minds with the Word of God that it soaks down into our hearts. When that happens, we *will not* sin against God. And make no mistake about it. When a man fails morally, the affront and offence is directly against God.

After his adultery, David cried out, *"Against thee, thee only, have I sinned, and done this evil in thy sight."*[8] The solution to this problem is simple in its distilled essence – significant absorption of the Word on a daily basis, 365 days a year. When that takes place, we will be primed to walk in the spirit. When that takes place, *we will* not sin against God.

As God directed Joshua to meditate in His Word day and night, so spiritual leaders need do so today, especially in this wicked and adulterous generation. Going to the Word day and night demands spending time therein during the day and in the evening at a minimum. But I wonder how many spiritual leaders actually do so?

Some years ago, I wrote a book entitled, *Training Your Children to Turn Out Right.*[9] In that book, I advanced the same principle for training children, to wit, they needed to be in the Word in the morning and before bedtime as a minimum. That, I believe, is the essence of being in the Word day and night. This was based again upon Joshua 1:8 and Psalm 1:3.

Not long thereafter, a spiritual leader of a prominent church, nationally known and heading an institution of higher learning, commented to me about being in the Word day and night. He thought that was quite novel. The only other time he said he had ever heard of such a practice was while on a missions trip and a native pastor mentioned that he followed the same practice.

I was amazed. Here was a spiritual leader, well-known across this nation and then some, who seemed oblivious to the principle of being in the Word day and night. I wondered if he had ever read Psalm 1 or Joshua 1. It surely was apparent he did not practice being in the Word day and night. I have no reason to question that man's integrity. As far as I know, he is blameless and above reproach. But his comments were revealing to me.

How many a lessor-known preacher is not in the Word in any significant degree? It is no wonder that men in spiritual leadership fail morally in this wicked and adulterous generation. Without the influence of the Word filling their minds and soaking into their hearts, they leave themselves open to the snare of the evil one.

With the multiplicity of ministries which many spiritual leaders oversee, not a few might confess that they don't have time to be in the Word day and night. They have a substantial church to pastor. They prepare sermons each week. They write lessons. They counsel people. They conduct staff meetings. They make visits. They have a substantial Christian school to oversee. They belong to state and national associations for both their church and their school. Accordingly, they travel to various association and fellowship meetings. They are on boards and committees of para-church organizations. Some are requested conference speakers. Some even write books. Not a few find time for the golf links each week. Last, but not least, they try and squeeze in some "quality time" with their wife and family.

"Spend time in the Word day and night? Read the Bible through several times a year? Are you kidding? I don't have time for that!"

And, the truth be told, they don't. Then we wonder why there is such a terrible litany of moral failure for those in spiritual leadership. Yet, one day, a man in spiritual leadership – some in high-profile, nationally-known places of leadership – will succumb to the temper's snare. Ironically, now they will have the time to be in the Word as they ought. But now they have no ministry, a lost reputation, suddenly no income, and their lives are wrecked.

My friends, this is not rocket science. God has provided a powerful, profound, yet simple means to keep one from falling. It is saturating our minds with the Word, yea day and night, to such a degree it soaks down into our hearts. When that happens, we *will not* sin against Him. We then will walk in the spirit and not fulfill the lust of the flesh. And, the devil will be unable to trip us up.

* * * * *

Casual Regard to the Principle of Righteousness

As described in Chapter 6 of this book, the principle of righteousness is spiritual armor.[10] A life ordered by the principle and practice of righteousness will say NO when the siren song of a temptress sings ever so sweetly. Character built upon doing what is right will say NO when the urge comes to sneak onto the internet and stare at harlots in pornographic poses. The habitual practice of always seeking to do what is right will preclude the temptation to flirt with some pretty little thing who catches one's eye.

A life built around doing what is right will be a powerful inhibition when the "gentlemen's club" looms on the road-side and nobody knows who you are in that part of town. When a woman telegraphs through body language and non-verbal communication that she is available and willing, a life ordered by righteousness will be armor on the right hand and on the left.

Yet, such conviction to do what is right comes from the Word of God and the new nature which was created in righteousness. They all interact and reenforce each other. We have come to a place in modern Christianity where we think that accountability groups, internet filters, and office doors with windows are the solution to the crisis of moral failure. While none of those things are wrong and in fact are good, the real solution must be internal. There must be a conviction to do right, regardless. That is uprightness.

Mike Morgan[11] was from a longstanding family of godly people. His grandfather was a well-known pastor and associational leader in years of yore. His father had been in the ministry his entire life. Mike, also headed into the ministry. He attended a well-known Christian college and was a student leader in various campus activities. Upon graduation he married and became an assistant pastor of a good church in a suburban area of a large city in the Southwest.

Part of his duties was directing the youth group of the church. One teenage girl took a particular liking to pastor Mike. She was attractive and already knew how to deport herself in a sensual way. Pastor Mike could not help but notice this cute, friendly, sometimes immodestly dressed girl who was pursuing him. One day, he could not resist the urge to touch her inappropriately to which she responded positively. The relationship degenerated into a sexual one of which the girl was a willing partner.

When discovered, not only did Pastor Mike lose his position and reputation, he was arrested and charged with sexual assault of a minor. As a result, he wound up spending time behind bars. What a sad and bitter end for a young man with good potential. The reasons? Only God will know the spiritual weaknesses which allowed him to make such a wrong decision, but one thing is for sure, he was not ordered by the principle of righteousness.

Weakness of Marriage Relationships

As noted earlier in this book, there is no justification for adultery or moral failure. None. However, a strong, healthy marriage relationship can be helpful in deflecting temptation. If the spiritual principles mentioned above are not in place, the protection of a solid marriage likely will only be minimal. Nevertheless, God has ordained for a godly wife to satisfy her husband's physical desires.

This is evident in I Corinthians 7:2 "*Nevertheless, to avoid fornication, let every man have his own wife, and let every woman have her own husband.*" As noted earlier, the word translated as "fornication" (πορνεια *porneia*) in this context encompasses the whole spectrum of moral failure, including adultery.

A godly wife who is a willing lover of her husband in the marriage bedroom very well can fortify her husband against the temptation of other women. Sweetness and satisfaction of marital intimacy, in large measure, is a function of an otherwise warm and loving marriage, spiritually and emotionally. Intimacy in bed is the icing on the cake of an otherwise happy marriage. Hence, a strong marriage both spiritually as well as sexually is basic protection against temptation.

Moreover, a wife who keeps herself slim, trim, and physically attractive can provide strong defense against her husband's natural (though sinful) curiosity of pornography. If a wife is attractive to look upon behind the closed doors of the marriage bedroom, a man will be less inclined to succumb to pornography.

Unfortunately, such frequently is not the case. It is not uncommon for a woman to ration intimacy to her husband as a carrot to get something she wants. Bickering, stubbornness, and fighting will also cool or sour what could otherwise be sweetness and satisfaction of marital intimacy. In some cases, Christian women have been influenced by the Augustinian philosophy that sexual relations even between a husband and wife are a necessary evil, only to be accomplished for procreation. Whatever the cause, when there is a coolness or infrequency of marital relations, a husband is more prone to be tempted. And, the devil knows that. The Apostle Paul in fact warned of this in I Corinthians 7:5.

Reverend Peterson[12] had been married for twenty-five years. Unfortunately, he had not had a happy marriage. He and his wife fought continually. He would be inconsiderate of her and she could lacerate him with her tongue. Furthermore, over the years, she did not take care of herself and had become obviously overweight. If it had ever entered her mind to be physically attractive to her husband, it was long forgotten. In their bedroom, he saw an overweight woman with flabby thighs. She was not attractive. In fact, the opposite might be thought.

One day, Reverend Peterson received an unsolicited email which caught his curiosity. When he clicked on it, it took him to a pornographic website. There, he saw everything he did not see in his bedroom at home. Though he was initially convicted, the lust of his flesh caused him to keep clicking from one pornographic picture to the next. Several days later, he succumbed to the temptation to find other pornographic sites. It wasn't hard.

On one pornographic website was an advertisement to meet "hot XXX rated women in your area." He clicked on the site and eventually got online with a cyber prostitute. Of course, it required a credit card number, which would be his undoing. To make a long story short, he was eventually discovered and his ministry was ruined. However, apart from spiritual principles discussed earlier, one can only wonder if Pastor Peterson would have succumbed to the temptation if his wife and marriage had been what they should have been.

Summary

Spiritual leaders fail morally because of spiritual deficiencies. Regardless of how much formal education a man has and regardless of how prominent a position he holds, if he is not walking in the spirit, he sooner or later may fulfill the lusts of the flesh. Men fail to walk in the spirit by (1) not crucifying their flesh on a daily basis. (2) They fail to walk in the spirit because of a lack of significant absorption of the Word of God in their hearts on a daily basis. Reading books of theology or current issues will never cause one to walk in the spirit (including this book).

Moreover, for many, their intake of the Word is in bite-sized portions in short "devotions." (3) Men fail because they do not pray without ceasing. Again, apart from the Word, there is no spiritual practice which will keep one walking in the spirit than prayer. When on the line with God, the devil can't get through. The line is busy! (4) Many fail because their day-to-day living is not ordered by the principle of righteousness. Again, this is the basic trait of the new nature. Finally, (5) weakness of marriage relationships can make a man more susceptible to temptation and the devil knows it. Once again, the issues of life are fundamentally spiritual.

Chapter Notes

[1]Matthew 12:39 and 16:4

[2]Hosea 4:11

[3]Galatians 5:19

[4]Galatians 5:16

[5]Proverbs 16:18

[6]Psalm 119:11 As noted earlier, the Hebrew grammar in the original text has the sense, "Thy word have I hid in mine heart, that I WILL not sin against thee."

[7]Luke 12:48

[8]Psalm 51:4

[9]David Sorenson, *Training Your Children to Turn Out Right* (Independence, MO: AACS, 1995)

[10]II Corinthians 6:17, Ephesians 6:14

[11]Once again, a fictitious name

[12]Of course, a fictitious name.

Chapter 9

Twelve Reasons to Resist Moral Failure

Moral failure, whether adultery, the lasciviousness of pornography, or some other form of sexual depravity, is sin. But it is also extremely destructive when committed by one in spiritual leadership. The consequences are profound and in most cases permanent. Accordingly, for one in spiritual leadership, sin of this nature is not only wrong, it is dumb – industrial-strength stupid. It is bad enough when Joe Nobody commits adultery or accumulates pornography. But when a pastor or other type of spiritual leader engages therein, it becomes a weapon of spiritual destruction.

By the grace of God, this author has not committed adultery or been a viewer of pornography, not to mention such abominations as homosexuality. I intend never to do so. I have assiduously sought to follow the advice given earlier in this book. However, on a more prosaic level, I from time to time remind myself of the consequences of succumbing to sexual sin or any other form of unrighteousness for that matter. Listed below are twelve reasons to resist moral failure. Each of them individually is cause enough to not yield to temptation. Collectively, they form a barrier which if trespassed is utterly stupid. In my view, upon considering these twelve reasons, one is not only wrong, but a fool to succumb to moral failure.

1. Ruin My Testimony

When one yields to the lust of the flesh for sexual sin, he will invariably ruin his testimony of Christ. One in spiritual leadership has been given a trust of representing Jesus Christ, whether the stewardship is a pastorate, college presidency, evangelist, or some other position of leadership. To succumb to adultery or consumption of pornography violates that trust. People in the church know it is wrong. They know it is a violation of Scripture. Even people in the world know that. When a spiritual leader yields to the lust of his flesh in this regard, he is announcing to all who find out that he is a hypocrite, two-faced, and deceitful.

Moreover, sexual sin, of all kinds of sin, has an amazing property for finding itself out, particularly when the guilty party is in spiritual leadership. The world loves scandal and when it involves a Bible-believing preacher, word travels fast. The warning of Moses remains, "*and be sure your sin will find you out.*"[1] When it is known, and it assuredly will be, the personal testimony of the guilty will be ruined for years to come, possibly forever. Mark it down. If one yields to such temptation, (a) he will eventually be found out and (b) his testimony will be ruined.

2. Grieve the Lord

Sin of any type grieves the Spirit of God. However, when an undershepherd, one entrusted with the spiritual influence and care of God's people, fails morally; how grieved must our Lord and His Spirit be? His reaction very well may also shift to disgust and then anger. David full well realized that his sin was against God and Him alone.[2] I, for one, would hate to be on the receiving end of His righteous indignation.

I am aware of at least one preacher who became an inveterate adulterer – literally a whoremonger. God took him. He killed him. I had the occasion to observe his lifeless body at the funeral home. The only thought which came to my mind was, "*and sin, when it is finished, bringeth forth death.*"[3] God may not chose to cause the premature death of every fallen spiritual leader. However, knowing what I knew about this situation, there was no question in my mind that this man had faced the wrath of God. God had had enough of his hypocrisy and He took him early. It is a fearful thing to fall into the hands of the living God.[4] Moreover, there is a sin unto death.[5]

3. Deeply Wound My Wife

In some sorry marriages, offending one's wife might not seem to be a big deal. But I can assure you that me yielding to sexual sin would deeply wound my dear wife. She would be heart broken. Her trust and love would be betrayed. She has faithfully stood by me all these years. She has been a faithful partner, helpmate, and lover. To get involved with another woman would break her heart. That is reason enough to stop this preacher from infidelity. Love is others' oriented. My love for my wife precludes me from seeing her utterly crushed. Moreover, adultery is a significant cause of many a divorce. Over the years, I have watched the gut-wrenching turmoil which follows most divorces. It leaves a trail of not only broken homes, but also tends to poverty financially.

Why wound my best friend? Why betray her trust? In the vast majority of adulterous relationships, there is not true love between the adulterers; only infatuation and gratifying the lust of the flesh. One is no fool to preserve the eternal warmth of a loving spouse for the fleeting gratification of a loose woman or shameless pictures of harlots.

4. Give Account at the Bema

When any Christian goes into sin, especially immorality, mark it down, he will give account thereof at the Judgment Seat of Christ. II John 8 intimates that sin can erase rewards one might otherwise receive in heaven.[6] I believe that sin will diminish rewards at the Bema. What a sad occasion. After having served Christ for many years, it will be bitter to have the rewards of that labor diminished by a brief season of sinful pleasure. This is true for any believer who is guilty of moral failure.

However, the Judgment Seat of Christ, I believe, will be a particularly bitter experience for one who was an undershepherd and failed morally. Unto whom much is given, much will be required. *"It is a fearful thing to fall into the hands of the living God."*[7] One to whom our Lord has entrusted a flock or other ministry and who damaged that work by his own carnal sin, I believe, will find the Bema a fearful experience.

In some cases, men have succumbed to traps of the devil. Others have succumbed in moments of weakness. And, I believe the Lord is merciful and will deal accordingly. Yet there are men in spiritual leadership who have engaged in immoral activities over long periods of time before eventually being found out. Their consciences were seared. In that day, I believe, they may face the wrath of the glorified Christ.

Saved? Apparently, yet so as by fire.[8] Their rewards in heaven will be few if at all.

To be quite candid, I fear someday standing before Jesus Christ and giving account. I am all too well aware of how I have failed Him over the years. I fear being rebuked by Him. I fear losing rewards which might have otherwise been won and that fear of the Lord constrains me to depart from evil.[9] When temptation swirls about, one must remember that he will someday give an account to the righteous judge. What chagrin and loss it will be for those who have chosen to pursue the lusts of the flesh in an immoral fashion.

5. Embarrass My Children

God has given this preacher two lovely daughters. They have been morally pure. What a terrible embarrassment it would be for me to face them if I pursued sinful lusts of the flesh. How could I face them? How diminished would I be in their eyes. As I have learned of sad and bitter moral failures of men in spiritual leadership across the land, I have often wondered how the failure of a father affected his children. In some cases, they may have been too young to understand the implications of it all. However, in other cases, such sin has devastated the older children of a fallen leader.

In at least one case of which I am aware, the children of the adulterous father not only turned their backs on their unrepentant father, most of them chose to have nothing to do with him thereafter. What was particularly sad was that this fallen leader no longer even saw his grandchildren. Every situation is different. In some cases, the guilty party is contrite and repentant, to his credit. Others are not. But the children of the guilty will be profoundly affected by their father's sin and it will never be for good.

Again, when the soft breezes of temptation arise, a man ought to consider how his sin will impact his children. Sooner or later, it will be found out. And his children will be wounded for life.

6. Damage to the Church and Young Christians

Moral failure always damages God's work. Churches are hurt. Young Christians are frequently disillusioned. Though there are varying types of moral failure and varying degrees of culpability, the church or institution the disgraced leader leaves behind is always wounded. In situations of which this writer has personal knowledge, young Christians simply gave up. They quit. What a tragedy! Older and more mature saints continued but were discouraged and disheartened. The outreach and testimony of the church in question usually comes to a screeching halt. Attendance, offerings, faith promise programs, and such like usually diminish as the church goes into a healing pattern which may takes years to accomplish.

When the leadership of an institution of higher learning is involved, there are young men preparing for the ministry who simply drop out. The spiritual aftermath is like unto the aftermath of a hurricane. Everything is damaged.

Men who have invested years into building a work will do long-term damage to what they have worked so long to build when they accede to the tempter's snare. Any preacher or spiritual leader had best consider that when contemplating fulfilling the lusts of the flesh.

7. Give the Devil a Victory

Throughout history, the evil one has always been the enemy. He has endlessly sought to damage or destroy God's work. In some periods of history, the devil has succeeded in bringing about such persecution that churches fail and Christians flee. In other cases, he has infiltrated churches and other Christian institutions such that apostasy has entered and the work dies from within spiritually. In other cases, the devil has succeeded in bringing the world into the church through the side door such that there is no longer much difference between the world and the church. Satan revels in Laodicean Christianity. And, yet when the devil cannot damage God's work through these means, he may find a crack in the ramparts of God's work through the weakness of the flesh in spiritual leaders.

Though individual leaders are ultimately culpable for their sin, they should realize that moral failure is part of a greater strategy of the devil. If the wicked one cannot destroy or damage God's work in one way, he will try another. Sadly, in this generation, there are too many preachers and spiritual leaders who have not adequately armed themselves against this device of the devil. We are witnessing the tragic consequences of this all across the land, even as we speak.

8. Loss of Position

When a spiritual leader fills his eyes with pornography or gets involved with another woman, he should realize that sooner or later he will lose his position. If he is a pastor, he soon will not be so. If he is a Bible college or seminary president, before long he will not be. Intangible damage such as a ruined testimony, reprimand at the Bema, or giving the devil a victory will eventually become quite tangible. Loss of a job, loss of a title, loss of a position, loss of an office (figuratively and literally) are very tangible results when a pastor or spiritual leader fails morally. A mechanic probably will not lose his position for having pornography on his computer, but a pastor will. A salesman probably will not lose his position for slipping into a strip club, but a spiritual leader will. An accountant probably will not lose his position for fooling around with another woman, but a pastor will.

The whole issue of moral failure is not a game, though the devil might have us think so. Some foolish people get a perverse thrill out of living one step ahead of being caught. They pride themselves in being too smart to be found out. And it is almost like a big game – sneaking around and fooling around with sin. Yet one day, they find out that it was no game when they are out of a position. Suddenly, they are just another guy out in a cold and cruel world. Their position is gone. Their influence is gone. Their reputation is gone. They sold their lives for a mess of pottage. And their number, sadly, has increased greatly.

9. Loss of Income

Those in spiritual leadership are like everyone else. They get a paycheck each pay period. It is their livelihood. It is how they support themselves and their family. There usually are fringe benefits as well: health insurance, retirement, sometimes a house in which they live. However, when a spiritual leader slides into moral failure, before long he will lose his paycheck, his health insurance, his retirement, and may have to move out of the house in which he lives. That is very tangible. The time spent staring at nude harlots on his computer screen are hardly worth the loss he will incur when he is found out. The fleeting moments of excitement and gratification in having an adulterous affair will never be worth the financial loss a spiritual leader will incur when found out. And be sure, your sin will find you out!

Sexual sin is industrial-strength stupid. Yet, men caught up in the lusts of their flesh will sacrifice their very livelihoods for the hollow pleasure of sexual sin. Failed leaders eventually find other work. But there will be a very difficult time of transition in between.

10. Loss of Career

A consequence similar to that above and yet of longer range is the loss of one's career. Most men in spiritual leadership have sacrificed to go to Bible college. They may have skimped to make it through seminary. They then have spent years in maturing a ministry of spiritual leadership. However, when they slide into sexual sin, their long-wrought career in the ministry will soon be over.

What is particularly sad about moral failure for one in spiritual leadership is that he nullifies any prospect for a future ministry. When a man in some other field has to leave town because of a moral scandal, he often can go elsewhere and start over again in his chosen field of endeavor. However, when a pastor or spiritual leader fails, it will be difficult at best and most likely impossible to ever be a pastor or hold position of spiritual leadership again. That may seem harsh, but that's the way it is.

Sexual sin follows a man in spiritual leadership. It is virtually impossible to keep such things secret. Invariably, a man's past in this regard will trail along after him. Even if he manages to hide his past from a pulpit committee and obtain another pulpit, sooner or later news of a past scandal will surface. Sexual sin is DUMB. It will destroy the life-long career of one in spiritual leadership. The prospects of such, if for no other reason, have helped this preacher say NO when opportunities for such sin have arisen.

11. Lose a Lifetime of Training and Experience

In similar fashion, when a spiritual leader yields to sexual sin, he is throwing away a lifetime of training and experience in the ministry. All of his schooling is essentially for naught. All of the valuable experience in the ministry becomes essentially moot. He has thrown away a lifetime for a mess of pottage. What a tragic waste! Of course, the devil knows that and chortles with glee. He has knocked off another servant of God. Apart from the human tragedy of a damaged or wrecked marriage, damage to a church and young Christians, a fallen spiritual leader has thrown away a valuable lifetime of further service to Jesus Christ. If he repents, God will forgive and he may be restored to fellowship as a church member; however, he will never again have the degree of ministry he once held.

12. Disgrace

Amidst all of the other untoward consequences of moral failure, the bottom line is disgrace. The preacher who fails morally is disgraced. His ministry is disgraced. His reputation is disgraced. His testimony is disgraced. His family is disgraced. What an ignoble end for one who started out years earlier to serve God in the gospel ministry. It is tragic and it is bitter.

Conclusion

The purview of this book has not been to deal with the fallen leader after the fact. Hopefully, those who do fail morally will repent of their sin, restore damaged family relationships, ask forgiveness of the ministry they disgraced, and go on in their Christian life. They will never have the stature they once held, but hopefully they can and will go on as a believer.

However, the purpose of this book is a warning to those about to go into the ministry or who are active in the ministry. That warning is of the perils of moral failure. Sadly, it is not just young men in the ministry who so fail. News accounts have surfaced of the bitter stories of men with decades of experience in God's work who have failed morally in recent years. If this book can prevent just one spiritual leader from moral failure, it will have been worth it all.

To summarize, this preacher has determined to avoid moral failure at all costs because it will ruin my testimony. It will grieve the Lord. It will deeply wound my wife. I will give account at the Judgment Seat of Christ. It will embarrass my children. It will damage the church and young Christians. It will give the devil a major victory. I will lose my position, my income, and my ministry, as well as a lifetime of training and experience. Finally, I will be disgraced.

I determined years ago that when the soft breezes of temptation come, the decision is already made. The answer is NO. There are a multitude of reasons for that as outlined in this book. It is my hope that readers of this volume, both younger as well as older, might determine to make the same decision in advance and prevent moral failure in their ministry.

Chapter Notes

[1]Numbers 32:23

[2]Psalm 51:4

[3]I have known more than one preacher who yielded to moral failure who died a premature death.

[4]Hebrews 10:31

[5]I John 5:16

[6]*"Look to yourselves, that we lose not those things which we have wrought, but that we receive a full reward*" 2 John 1:8.

[7]Hebrews 10:31

[8]I Corinthians 3:15

[9]Proverbs 16:6 "*And by the fear of the LORD men depart from evil.*"